Managing Difficult Employees

by Joseph Koob

Copyright © 2008 by Joseph E. Koob II

ISBN 0-7414-4661-8

For more information address inquiries to
responses2@difficultpeople.org

or visit
www.difficultpeople.org.

A difficultpeople.org publication

Published by:

PUBLISHING.COM

1094 New DeHaven Street, Suite 100
West Conshohocken, PA 19428-2713
Info@buybooksontheweb.com
www.buybooksontheweb.com
Toll-free (877) BUY BOOK
Local Phone (610) 941-9999
Fax (610) 941-9959

Printed in the United States of America

Printed on Recycled Paper

Published March 2008

The WORK Trilogy

By Dr. Joseph E. Koob

Succeeding with Difficult Coworkers

Succeeding with Difficult Bosses

Managing Difficult Employees

Available on-line at www.DifficultPeople.org

and major on-line book retailers.

PART I
KNOW YOURSELF

Preface

Chapter 1	Management, Leadership, People	1
Chapter 2	People Management	9
Chapter 3	Leadership	15
Chapter 4	Integrity, Ownership, Responsibility	23
Chapter 5	Caring	29
Chapter 6	Walk, Listen, Learn, Follow-Up	33
Chapter 7	Bureaucracy	41
Chapter 8	Time Management	47
Chapter 9	Keys to Boss – Employee Communications	55
Chapter 10	Self-Awareness	63
Chapter 11	Self-Worth	69
Chapter 12	Self-Confidence	75
Chapter 13	Self-Control	79
Chapter 14	Honesty	83
Chapter 15	Kindness and Compassion	91
Chapter 16	Positivity	97
Chapter 17	Taking Care of Your People	103
Chapter 18	Taking Care of Yourself	111

PART II
MANAGING DIFFICULT EMPLOYEES

Chapter 19	Difficult Employees	119
Chapter 20	Communicating in Difficult Situations	129
Chapter 21	Moody, Depressed	141
Chapter 22	Whining, Complaining, and General Negativity	149
Chapter 23	Mediation	157
Chapter 24	Incompetent, Unmotivated, Under-achieving	165
Chapter 25	Aggressive, Rude, Obnoxious	171
Chapter 26	Passive-Aggressive Surreptitious Behaviors	177
Chapter 27	Passive Behavior	185
Chapter 28	Ambitious, Obsequious	189
Chapter 29	Prejudice, Discrimination, Bias, Sexual Harassment	193
Chapter 30	Really Difficult Behaviors	209
Chapter 31	Leading By Example	215
Appendix I	Handling Employee Evaluations	217
Appendix II	Being in Control	225
Appendix III	Annotated Bibliography	229
Bibliography		235

Managing Difficult Employees

Preface

This book is written from a grass-roots perspective of how you as a manager work with and lead 'your people'*, i.e., what you need to know and what skills you bring to the table that address two key questions:

> What can I do as a manager and leader to create a work environment that fosters positive personnel development?
>
> In other words, <u>preventive maintenance</u> – avoiding difficult people concerns and difficult situations through competent management and inspired leadership

And,

> What foundation of knowledge do I need, and what skills can I learn to be able to deal with concerns that are present or that may arise?

Starting from a premise that you are consistently working on your management and leadership skills, and even more importantly, that you CARE about the people who work for you, this book will focus on key areas that foster positive personnel and team development. You set the stage through your example, through your management style, and through what you are willing to put up with relevant to how people interact, how they produce, and how they feel at work.

*Your People

My Dad, a career army officer and subsequently a bank Vice President always talked about 'his people.' It wasn't a mark of possession, but an indication of his deep and abiding concern for who they were and how they were doing. If Dad said, "I have to get down to the bank today and sign the payroll checks so my people get paid before the holidays," he was going that extra mile, which meant 'his people' mattered more than his Saturday morning. In other words, he cared.

What you will Learn

The first part of this book is about knowing <u>yourself</u>. Then we will focus on how you can use that self-knowledge to understand how things you do and say impact your employees. We will touch on key management and leadership ideas that help foster a positive growth environment for you and your team members. If you are a new manager and still learning basic skills, I encourage you to read as much about leadership as you can and commit yourself to a program of learning, self-understanding, and improvement as long as you are in a leadership role.

[See the extensive Bibliography for many excellent sources on Management and Leadership. My books, *Honoring Life and Work: 99 Words for Leaders to Live By* and *Leaders Managing Change*, offer a rich foundation to jump off from – available at www.difficultpeople.org, and major on-line retail stores.]

Part II of this work will demonstrate how to apply your personal strengths and your management and leadership skills to working successfully with difficult personnel concerns and with difficult situations that may arise.

[The 'Difficult People' Bibliography at the end of this book offers extensive suggested readings. My books, *Succeeding with Difficult Coworkers* and *Succeeding with Difficult Bosses* offer unique and focused perspectives of other relationships in the workplace.]

The onus, as a manager and as a leader, is on you being successful with your team members. What you bring to the table makes all the difference in the world.

Approaching this Book

The knowledge and skills discussed in this book build from chapter to chapter. Your best learning will result by working through the entire text and then returning to areas that are particularly relevant to your situation.

Each chapter includes a brief section at the end entitled, "Questions and Ideas for Contemplation." These ideas and exercises are designed for personal growth and are highly recommended. Working through these materials can give you added insight.

Thanks

To the difficult people I have had in my life for 'driving' me toward this adventure.

Most especially thanks to the usual cast of characters: Anne D., my primo editor; Nathan, Lisa, and Kay for your input, and Arwen (my dog) whose insistence on long walks often created the time needed to contemplate an important point.

PART I

Know Yourself

Nosce Te Ipsum

Chapter 1

Management, Leadership, People

Key Ideas

Management is the...

"Process of coordinating organizational resources to meet a goal."

(Rachman, et al)

Your most important resources are the people who work for you. Making sure they are on the bus and in the right seats is probably one of the most challenging management tasks you will face. (Collins; Peters). However, if you can accomplish this, you will very likely have far fewer personnel concerns in the long run.

Your employees want to be content with what they are doing and they want to feel they are contributing in key ways. Making an effort to understand who they are and what is important to them helps build their personal commitment to who you are and what is important to you and the organization.

'People management' means being concerned that your team members are not only good at what they do, but are content (if not down-right happy) doing it. This takes not only intelligent management, but you also have to be a supportive, inspiring leader. When you understand how you come across to others, i.e. the impact you have on them on a daily basis, you have a powerful key component of quality people management.

Leadership is the...

> "Skill of persuading others to achieve organizational goals
>
> by showing how things are done
>
> and by setting an example in behavior and spirit."
>
> (Rachman, et al)

Much of this book is about leadership; which, in turn, is all about applying your knowledge and skills in such a way that your team members care about what they are doing and how they are doing it. It is also about your team members **knowing** that you care about what they are doing, how they are doing it, and most importantly that you care about them.

Five Key Leadership Qualities you NEED to have

(from *Honoring Work and Life: 99 Words for Leaders to Live By*, Koob)

Integrity

How do you perceive yourself? – Your personal integrity?

How do others perceive you?

> Do they trust you?
>
> Believe you?
>
> Appreciate who you are and how you do things?

If they don't, you have personal work to do.

How do you perceive others?

> Do you trust your team members?
>
> Do you believe in them?
>
> Do you know who they are and what they do?
>
> Do you understand what motivates them?
>
> Do you appreciate, acknowledge, and recognize them for their efforts

Honesty

Honesty is more than telling the truth; it also means being open to the truth. Being honest is the foundation for trust and for open communications – Trust is the foundation for Integrity.

It is not enough to tell the truth when it is convenient and to avoid speaking when it is not. Honesty means being able and willing to tell the truth in the most difficult of circumstances.

Ownership

Do you 'own up' to…

>   Your life

>   Your work?

>   The decisions you make?

>   The decisions your team members make?

Or do you blame, complain, pass-the-buck, and otherwise avoid difficult problems and concerns?

Ownership is about taking responsibility (see below) for your life and work. When we 'own' something we have the power to change it, to make something of it, and when there is a problem, the ability to find solutions.

Responsibility

As a manager and a leader you assume a great deal of responsibility –

>   First, to yourself

>   Then, to your team members, individually and collectively

>   To your organization

>   To anyone and everyone that your position influences throughout your work day

When we assume responsibility we have the opportunity and obligation to find solutions. It does not work well any other way.

An important leadership perspective worth remembering is:

When you accept responsibility for a problem,

you have a much better chance of finding a solution –

even if you don't feel the problem originates with you.

You don't have to accept blame – just responsibility to DO SOMETHING!

Taking responsibility is a form of
PERSONAL EMPOWERMENT

Caring

True leaders care for:

> How they lead others

> What they do and say and how that impacts others

> The entire scope of their job and its responsibilities

> The people they work with

> The people they work for

> Most especially, the people who work for them

Caring is a personal commitment to excellence. It is a commitment not only to others, but to yourself. When you care, you can make a difference in the lives of other people.

You will also make an amazing difference in your own life and work!

Bravery

I added this one at the last minute, but it hit me that a key leadership quality, one that really does make a difference, is our willingness to jump into the fray when it is needed. It is an especially important quality when we find it necessary to go to bat for our employees.

The best managers and leaders I have known have been the ones I felt not only cared about me as a person, but who were willing to go that extra mile for me if I asked for it or if it was needed.

It takes a good bit of courage to be a leader.

Managing by Numbers

It is far more cost effective, both financially and psychologically, to solve difficult employee concerns than to deal with the frustrations and legal issues surrounding 'letting someone go.'

It is even more cost effective to create a personal approach and team atmosphere that encourages positive interpersonal dynamics and limits the potential for personnel problems to develop from the get-go.

You will save everyone time and effort as well.

Managers and businesses often avoid providing inspiring and practical training for executives as well as hiring executive coaches because of the high cost.

Saving just one talented, and yet disgruntled/unproductive employee through quality management and training is far cheaper than the costs associated with separation, legal issues, a lawsuit, etc.

MBWA – Management By Wandering Around

Tom Peters (and Nancy Austin – *In Search of Excellence*) has been shouting this mantra for decades, but for some reason many managers just don't seem to get it.

I believe MBWA means getting out amongst your team members with no other purpose in mind than to get to know them as people and to know what is important to them at work. Add anything else to the mix and you defeat the purpose, which is all about personnel development and team building. (See Chapter 6 for my take on this key technique – "Walk, Listen, Learn, Follow-up")

The Seven Keys to Being Successful with Difficult People

Self-Awareness

Self-worth

Self-confidence

Self-control

Honesty

Kindness

Positivity

These are all centered in 'How YOU approach other people' – specifically difficult employees, BECAUSE,

"You can only change yourself;

you cannot change other people...directly."

(Understanding and Working with Difficult People, Koob)

Your best opportunity for working through concerns with a difficult employee is to affect change by being a leader, i.e. to set a positive example based in these key skill areas.

[Dr. Koob's many books centered around "Understanding and Working with Difficult People," have fostered these seven Key Ideas. See Chapters 9 -15]

Communications

Open and positive communication amongst all personnel at all levels is critical to good management and high-quality leadership. You set the stage by your example and by what you are willing to accept from others whatever the forum: person-to-person; committees, meetings, speeches, e-mails, phone, etc.

Communicating in difficult situations with difficult people takes an open and positive approach a step further by learning the skills and techniques that help diffuse volatility and negativity.

Bureaucracy

You do have to know how to deal with it, but you don't have to create any more of it. Both these are important considerations in maintaining an open, constructive team atmosphere.

Take CARE of your People

When you take care of the people who work for you, they will help you in many ways. When you have the courage to stand up for them despite adversity, you will earn their respect and trust. Keep these points in mind whenever you make decisions that affect others.

Take Care of YOU

If you don't, everyone will suffer. This should be a no-brainer – unfortunately, far too often we ignore our own well-being and in the long run this affects everyone we work with.

Difficult People/Difficult Situations

Regardless of your best efforts, concerns will arise. Are you up for the challenge?

By knowing yourself, your management style, your personal foundation for leadership, you set the stage for being successful in difficult situations. The only other key step is understanding how specific employee difficulties can be successfully dealt with, which is what Part II of this book is all about.

Questions and Ideas for Contemplation

Part I of this book is about understanding yourself and how you approach things. The Key Ideas presented in this Introductory Chapter set the stage for learning more about who you are as a manager and leader and how your approach impacts your team members.

Above we have discussed five key attributes of a leader. Can you pick five others that you feel are key to your own leadership style? Write these down and then work out a paragraph or two as to why you feel these qualities are important to you and your success. [At the end of Chapter 3, "Leadership," we will present an exercise designed to consider this in even more detail.]

Chapter 2

People Management

"Process of…"

People management is an ongoing process. It is not simply putting people in a spot, having them do a certain task, and then expecting them to shine. It includes making sure they are content in that spot, and ensuring that they are doing a good job at whatever tasks they are expected to perform. For a manager it is a continuous process of recognizing what is happening and what is not happening, and then making adjustments based on how their people are doing.

"coordinating…"

Coordination presumes that things/people interrelate. When it comes to relationships between people at all levels in a team and organization, it means being aware of how those relationships are working – because if they are not working well, whatever your bottom line is, it is going to suffer. Difficult people within a team and organization can disrupt how things get done and they can affect many relationships both up and down the line and across matrices.

"organizational…"

It is rare these days that a business is mono-dimensional. Today managers have to deal with line personnel, matrix personnel, and a wide variety of other coworkers, managers, and employees who fit in the seams. Your success is predicated by how well you manage these many relationships. It is not just about staying in touch; it is very much about HOW you stay in touch.

"resources…"

People are your most important resource. One can manage a team or office quite efficiently without ever concerning oneself with people. Managed people might be efficient; they might even have decent productivity. What they won't have is much FUN. And you can be pretty well assured that their employees down the line are not going to be happy campers either.

To manage people well you have to get them doing what they are good at in a job they enjoy, in a setting that is conducive to their success, with the materials and support they need to be successful.

To lead people you need to do all of the above and also care about who they are, how they are doing, and how they feel. And then you need to show it by acknowledging them for who they are, appreciating them for what they accomplish on a daily basis, and recognizing and rewarding them for everything that goes above and beyond.

"to meet a goal."

Management is "the process of coordinating organizational

resources to meet a goal."

(Rachman, et al)

It's the bottom line!

It IS the bottom line. But ask yourself this every day:

Which is better?

To improve the bottom line whatever the cost?

Or

To improve the bottom line while everyone on your team enjoys the process?

Both of these are usually feasible; one is just a lot more fun than the other – for them AND for you.

If you are not having FUN, something's wrong...adjust.

(Koob, *Understanding and Working with Difficult People*)

If **they** are not having any fun, you better adjust because you are in for some people concerns – if your team members are not enjoying their work, problems will develop between people. That is pretty much guaranteed.

Get the Right People on the Bus and get them in the Right Seats (Collins)

You rarely have a choice about all of the people who are on your team. You often don't even have a choice, or at least not a very easy one, about getting someone off your team who is not working out. What you DO often have, is a certain amount of flexibility in getting people into a position where they can make a contribution.

Getting a person into the right seat means understanding who they are. This means getting to know who they are not just on paper, but what they care about, what is important to them, what gets them excited, what they are good at, and what they want. (See Chapter 6, "Walk, Listen, Learn, and Follow-Up")

Unfortunately it is not unusual in a business for a senior manager to slam someone into an open spot for convenience sake, rather than for all the right reasons. Putting someone on the wrong bus and in the wrong seat is a lose-lose proposition the vast majority of times. It pays to find out:

> What knowledge-base and expertise they bring to the team
>
> How good they are at actually doing X, Y, and Z
>
> What they are interested in
>
> What they are passionate about
>
> What type of position they work well in and what type of people they work well with
>
> What they expect from a job, an opportunity, an assignment
>
> How they 'fit'

You can do this by looking at their resume, talking with their colleagues/former bosses, having them take a battery of tests, inventories, and so on. And certainly these are often good managerial tools that are at your disposal. They are often worth doing.

Unfortunately, far too often, even good managers forget the simplest knowledge-gaining process of them all – **ask them**. (Or, most unfortunately, if a manager remembers to ask, he/she ignores the person's input.)

Asking is one of the best communication tools you have – use it, and then listen carefully. You will probably learn far more than you ever thought you would about your people – about what drives them and about what makes them happy. When you use this information to the best advantage of your team, productivity will increase across the board, and so will your bottom line.

If there is no fit

Sometimes difficulties, even major concerns, arise between people because someone is on the bus who just does not fit into the team and where the bus is headed. As a manager and leader you still have to deal with them, or get rid of them – which as we all know can be a long, difficult, and expensive process in today's business climate.

Mentoring, coaching, supporting, training, etc., are tools any good manager needs to develop and use regularly. The more you use and develop these skills, the better you will become at fitting square pegs into less than square holes. Sometimes it requires some reshaping of the individual – training and support; sometimes it can mean reshaping the position they need to assume.

Is it worth making this effort? You always have a choice between accepting what is or making changes. Equanimity in the workplace can make a huge difference to everyone's ability to produce, and more importantly, to feel productive.

> Author's note: I have never been involved in a mentoring or coaching situation with a 'difficult' client or the manager of a 'difficult' employee where the situation could not be dramatically improved. It does take effort, support, encouragement, and patience, but it has always been well worth the effort and money spent. Much of the rest of this book discusses ideas, skills, and tools you can use to make a difference with people who tend to create difficult circumstances.

Create Opportunities for Success

You, as a manager and leader, are the key to solving people concerns. Recognize the problem – seek solutions. This is a cut-and-dried management approach, EXCEPT that we are talking about people. Add your concern and attention to the mix and you have the potential for a winning formula. You have to decide what skills and tools work the best for you and what may work with this specific circumstance/person.

When you make this effort,

you will bring yourself up from simply managing people,

to leading them.

Questions and Ideas for Contemplation

Have you…

Ever been in a job that just didn't suit you?

Ever had to work with people with whom you didn't meet eye-to-eye?

Ever feel over-your-head?

There are a lot of reasons people have difficulties at work. Part of your management task is to find out the root causes of concerns and to make every effort to address them.

Often simply the active involvement of a manager in trying to solve a difficult situation helps change the dynamics of the situation a great deal. Taking that involvement one step further by helping lead them through changes that need to be made might be the one catalyst that effects positive differences for them at work.

Chapter 3

Leadership

"...setting an example in behavior and spirit."

(Rachman)

What does leadership mean to you?

When you can answer this question thoroughly and with conviction, you are ready to lead others. Until that time, you have work to do.

PLUS!

And this is a very key point – **leadership is a process**. You don't just 'get there' and then you are a great leader; **you keep becoming**.

Great leaders commit to learning;

learning from the people they lead and are responsible for.

Take the Challenge

At the end of this chapter are the 99 words discussed in my book, *Honoring Life and Work, 99 Words for Leaders to Live By*. In the first chapter of this book five words from this list were discussed very briefly (Integrity, Honesty, Ownership, Responsibility, and Caring), giving you a perspective of the importance of assuming responsibility for who you are as a leader. These terms, and others, will be discussed at more length as this work progresses, but the current challenge is for you to do the recommended exercise at the end of this chapter using these 99 words as a jumping off point (see "Questions and Ideas for Contemplation").

The purpose of this challenge is for you to begin a foundation of understanding the ideas, values, and qualities that YOU feel are the most significant to your development as a top-notch leader.

Please note, that the list of ninety-nine words is not exhaustive. If you think of other terminology that better emphasizes your leadership approach and beliefs, add them. This is your list – this is YOU!

I highly recommend that you complete this challenge exercise right now, before continuing with this book. It will help you solidify your thoughts before continuing with your understanding of the skills and tools you can bring to difficult people concerns and difficult situations at work. Your own personal leadership style may also reflect other key ideas that help you focus on doing your best.

Discover who you are and who you want to be – then you can lead.

"My People/Your People"

My Dad was the ultimate people person – a consummate glad-hander. He always had something nice to say to everyone. As a career military officer and later a bank executive he managed and led people most of his adult life. I often heard him use the phrase, "My people" when he was referring to his staff. "A couple of my people are involved in this Diabetes Campaign and I want to make sure they have the bank's support."

This wasn't a phrase Dad used to show he was 'above' someone else or to show he was powerful and in-control of others; it was his commitment to others, his responsibility as a leader. It meant that Dad cared about his people and that he would bend over backwards to do the right thing when it was called for.

Dad was not an easy boss. He expected the best from his people and from himself. He did not put up with poor quality work and he expected things to be done on time (or before!). He drove himself the same way. But his people also knew that he was there FOR THEM and that he would make whatever effort it took to do things right – to do the best he could for his team and for each of them as individuals.

The ultimate statement from this type of leadership was seen at my Dad's funeral. He lived in a small town, yet even though it was Mother's Day and High School graduation weekend with many people away with their families, the line at his viewing was nonstop for four hours. At his funeral, people for whom he had served as a leader from decades earlier came and spoke. His people showed up.

What kind of legacy are you going to leave as a leader?

Keep in mind – it is not so much about your leadership style, the rules you follow, or the higher-ups you please, there are many, many different approaches you can take as a manager.

It is about the difference you make to the people

for whom you work – your employees.

Leadership is what you make of it

Ultimately leadership is about people. Ask yourself this question frequently:

How would I want to be led ...in this circumstance, in this situation?

Ask yourself this question especially when times are tough, or when you are dealing with a difficult situation/difficult person. Taking this small step back mentally changes your perspective and creates the opportunity to make positive choices for everyone involved.

If you have a leader you admire, or a mentor who you hope you could live up to, then ask this question:

What would _____ do with this concern, in this situation?

Or:

How would _____ handle this problem?

Leading through difficult times and Leading 'difficult people'

Certainly people can be very exasperating at times. Hard times and negative people can bring out the worst or best in us – **our choice**.

The rest of this book will help prepare you for making the best choices. However, keep in mind this important fact –

> **Regardless** of their (the perpetrator,
>
> difficult person, antagonist, etc.) behavior,
>
> YOU are the catalyst for what happens next.

Difficulty can manifest in many ways at work:

Relationships between people

Between coworkers

Between employee and boss

Cliques and intrigue

Across lines, matrices, divisions, etc.

Poor productivity

Poor quality work

Lack of motivation

Disruptive behavior

General negativity/doom and gloom

Whining, complaining, blaming

Resistance

And many other ways (see Part II of this book)

First and foremost you set the stage for handling difficulties by who you are and how well you understand who you are. Knowledge is a very powerful tool, and the most important knowledge you bring to the equation of "Understanding and Working with Difficult People" is knowledge of yourself.

Know who you are as a leader; understand at the deepest level what values and qualities you hold close, then bring these to the table, and you will have established a firm foundation upon which to lead through difficulties.

Questions and Ideas for Contemplation

A Challenge to you:

Immediately below you will find a list of 99 words initially published with discussion in Dr. Koob's book, *Honoring Work and Life: 99 Words for Leaders to Live By.* You can use this list as a jumping off place for understanding who you are as a leader and what is most important to you. This list is by no means exhaustive and you may find other words or phrases that better exemplify the ideas and values you hold close to your heart. Change/add anything that reflects who you are and what you value.

As a starting place, take this list and circle the values/qualities that 'jump out' at you, i.e. those you feel are closest to who you are and how you want to be – how you want to be perceived. Add words to the list as you think of things that seem to work better for you. Your goal is to focus on the values you feel are most important to you in your development as a leader.

After your initial time through the list, begin to organize your choices in any way you wish. Ultimately you want to focus on your top ten (or so) most important values/qualities. Once you have this top ten list, then if you wish, see if you can order them in some priority sequence. It is not necessary to do this, but this can also be enlightening. Are there one or two terms that stand out above the rest?

The next part of this exercise is to take your final top ten list (or fifteen, whatever works best for you) and write about each choice. Use a separate file/piece of paper for each term or phrase and just write – whatever comes to mind about this concept. The more freely and openly you can do this, the better. Let your feelings and thoughts roam about these terms. When you are done, set them aside and then in a day or so, or a week, come back and write some more. Keep doing this until you have had your say. [Hint: It is a good idea to come back to these files every so often – once a month, once a year – and revisit your thoughts. See how you have changed and whether you want to add anything more or see if your perspective has changed.]

If you complete this challenge exercise, you will have a good foundation and understanding of what is important to you. You may think you know; but you will likely be very surprised if you make this effort, because you will open yourself up a great deal in personal understanding with this process.

Another great suggestion is to type up your final list of terms and laminate a few copies. Keep one in your wallet, another by your computer, and another on your wall. These will prove a constant reminder of who you want to be and how you want to lead.

It doesn't hurt to remind ourselves frequently, especially when dealing with difficulties.

99 Words for Leaders to Live By

INTEGRITY

1. Integrity
2. Honesty**
3. Trust
4. Ownership
5. Accountable
6. Responsibility
7. Reliability
8. Self-control**
9. Loyalty
10. Committed
11. Conscientious
12. Credible
13. Stability
14. Continuity
15. Disciplined
16. Humility
17. Idealism

SERVICE to Others

18. Service
19. Appreciation
20. Acknowledgment
21. Respect
22. Courteous
23. Attention
24. Support
25. Grateful (Thanking People)
26. Recognition
27. Celebration
28. Ceremony
29. Reward

HONORING the Humanity of Others

30. Caring
31. Kindness**

32. Empathy
33. Compassion
34. Patience
35. Generous
36. Responsiveness
37. Grace

PERCEPTION

38. Self-awareness**
39. Awareness
40. Visibility
41. Connecting
42. Modeling

SELF-VALUE

43. Self-worth**
44. Self-respect
45. Self-confidence**
46. Character
47. Identity

QUALITY

48. Quality
49. Value-added
50. Stretching
51. Learning
52. Education
53. Renewal

54. Solution-focused
55. Catalyst
56. Cultivate
57. Rigorous

PERSONAL APPROACH

58. Persistence
59. Synthesizer
60. Cohesion
61. Attitude
62. Consistent
63. Cooperative
64. Competent
65. Discerning
66. Focus
67. Organized
68. Engagement
69. Determined
70. Energy
71.Down-to-earth
72. Simplicity

FREE YOURSELF

73. Creativity
74. Innovation
75. Flexibility
76. Experiment
77. Risk-taking

78. Fluidity

79. Chances

80. Imagination

81. Friction-free

82. Anticipates

83. Facilitates

84. Curiosity

85. Initiative

86. Choices

LIVE LIFE OUT LOUD

87. Passion

88. Vision

89. Conviction

90. Courage

91. Fearless

92. Zany

93. Spontaneous

94. Zesty

95. Intensity

96. Charisma

97. Showmanship

98. Positivity**

99. Symbolizes

**The Seven Keys to Understanding and Working with Difficult People

Chapter 4

Integrity, Ownership, Responsibility

Five key leadership concepts that have a marked impact on employee relations were discussed briefly in Chapter 1. In the next few chapters these will be delineated further in order to provide a solid foundation for understanding and managing difficult people concerns at work.

Do you have integrity?

Part of the work in the previous chapter was to help you root yourself in the values and qualities that are most important to you as a leader. When you live these values, you have personal integrity. You are 'in integrity.' (Perkins)

> Well...at least from your own personal perspective.

What about the perspective of others?

When employees consider who you are on a daily basis, what do they see?

> Do they see a person they trust?

> Do they feel you care?

> What are the most important facets of leadership that they consider in drawing a conclusion about your integrity?

Do you step up to the plate?

One thing every employee watches for in a leader is whether they are willing to go to bat for their employees. There are many attributes that reflect on this perspective – trust, ownership, responsibility, caring, etc. – but the bottom line is that your employees want to feel like **you** will be willing to make that extra effort on their behalf when the going gets tough.

> Author's Note: I have worked with many executives and managers over the years in a wide variety of roles – from

employee, to boss, to executive and personal coach, to mentor, to Department Head, to Department Heads' liaison to the Vice President and President. I have seen great managers and overall quite competent leaders, who, when push came to shove did not step-up-to-the-plate' for their employees if they felt they had to go up against senior management in any way. As a result, over the long haul, their integrity with employees suffered. Trust was lost. Concerns and problems deepened.

People expect you to fight the good fight. They don't always expect you to win. They expect you to try. They understand management and especially upper management better than you might think. They also are very observant when it comes to how you do things. Do not expect to get away with matters of integrity.

Trust

As a leader you garner trust through what you say (your ability to communicate openly and honestly are fundamental to this) and by what you do. They will notice even the small things. Many ideas and skills in this book come back to the development of trust, and trust is the foundation for your integrity with your employees. As you go through the rest of this book, keep this idea in mind.

You are not just learning basic ideas and skills that help you deal with this situation or that problem. You are building a foundation of knowledge that builds upon your skills as a leader and on the perception of you as a trusted leader who has integrity.

Trusting others

Integrity and trust are not just one way streets. When you can find ways to trust your team members and to give them ownership and responsibility without watching over their shoulders – you have come a long way toward personal trust and integrity with them. Sometimes this is the hardest lesson for managers to learn -- otherwise competent and skilled managers cannot keep their fingers out of the pie long enough for their employees to grow. It is most often perceived as micro-managing and is very frustrating to employees. It is especially exasperating to those who thrive on challenges and who hope to grow into leadership positions themselves.

If you want to be trusted, trust others.

If you want to have integrity in their eyes, see their own integrity and/or help them develop it –

That is leadership!

Ownership

Take ownership of <u>every</u> problem and concern that crosses your plate. Because when you do, you have the power to find solutions and to change things for the better. If you don't, you will soon find that you are powerless because the consensus of opinion will likely be that you foist everything onto others' shoulders.

Owning something, does not mean you have to accept negative responsibility (guilt) for 'the way it is." It does mean accepting responsibility to make it better! Taking ownership does not necessarily mean taking blame, either, though you should accept blame if it is at all warranted.

Ownership is about making everything in your purview important. You don't have to do it all. You don't have to pile everything on your own shoulders. However, you do have to be willing to take some of the load and the responsibility when it is needed. You also have to let people know the importance you attach to what, why, who, how, when, etc. They expect you to lead, to show the way, to help when things get tough, or provide support and assistance when something happens that they can't handle.

Most importantly – own who you are. [See previous chapter and Chapter 9)

Also, be sure to let them own who **they** are – their own jobs and responsibilities. Just be ready to lead –support, help, mentor, and guide whenever needed.

> Keep in mind that NEED is not necessarily when you <u>think</u> you should jump in, but more often, when you are <u>asked</u> to jump in. This is a very important distinction. When in doubt – ask. They will almost invariably tell you if they feel they can't handle something. Understanding people's personalities and approach to work will help you make this distinction further. (See Part II of this book)

Responsibility

Taking responsibility for who you are, what you do and what you say are keys to good leadership. While we all like to think we know ourselves well, most often we all have a great deal more we can learn, especially about how others see us (see Chapter 9, "Do You Know Yourself?"). The better you understand who you are and how you come across to others, the more you will be able to bring the best of who you are to the table.

Responsibility and Ownership are closely linked. People notice when we are responsible for things. They especially notice when we are willing to take responsibility in spite of 'whose fault it is.'

As a manager and leader you have many responsibilities. What your employees and fellow coworkers do notice is how you handle your responsibilities and most importantly your willingness to make the best effort possible to handle them. Failure does not matter as much as the failure to try, i.e., failure, in their eyes, of you to live up to what they see as your responsibilities, especially to them as employees and team members.

Don't assume people understand who you are and what you are about. Many managers have roles that take them far away from the trenches for far too much of the time. What they don't see and don't hear from the horse's mouth, they will fill in. A very important skill to develop is being open, willing, and consistent in providing your team with knowledge about you, what is important to you, to them, to the organization, and so on. Sometimes you have to say it, as well as show it:

> This is who I am.
>
> This is what I hold important.
>
> This is what we are about.

Then be willing to reiterate all of these on a regular basis.

When they are clear about what is important; what makes a difference to you, the team, their livelihood, etc., they will be willing to stand up for that and be willing to work toward it.

It also can be important to share what you are **not** about and what is **not** important. When people know; they rarely are willing to waste time and effort on something that will not benefit themselves or others.

Openness in communication is perhaps the single most important skill that helps you build your team's vision of who you are as a leader and manager – your integrity, trust, ownership, responsibilities. It helps show that you care. It is also critical to succeeding with difficult people concerns and difficult situations that arise.

Questions and Ideas for Contemplation

Answer these questions for yourself – writing your answers out can be very illuminating:

> What does integrity mean to you?
>
> How do you judge another person's integrity?
>
> What do you think is important to an employee in placing their trust in you?
>
> > A difficult employee?
>
> What do you look for in trusting an employee?
>
> How well do you rate yourself on owning problems that surface within your purview at work?
>
> > How would your employees rate you?
>
> Are you responsible?
>
> Do your employees see you as a responsible person?
>
> > Why?
> >
> > Why not?

Chapter 5

Caring

"If you are in a leadership position and you can't or won't care

for the people you work with and for,

then get out.

You might be a manager, but you will never be a leader."

(Koob, *Leaders Managing Change*)

Beyond Stepping up to the Plate

People expect you, as a manager and leader, to go to bat for them. They will appreciate whatever efforts you make for them and they will respect your integrity, ownership, and responsibility. But if you want them to care about who you are, what you believe in, what you stand for and what is important to you then you have to care about who they are, what they believe in, and what is important to them.

If you want them to see you as a great leader –

you have to care.

No, you don't have to get all mushy, over-sensitive, and touchy-feely. You <u>do</u> need to let them know, in a wide variety of ways, that they matter – that the bottom line is not the only thing driving who you are and what you are about.

There are many ways to show this, but the key really is in who you are, hence the strong quote at the beginning of this chapter. Self-examination is the first step in getting in touch with the person you are bringing to the leadership table. (See Challenge exercise in chapter 3, "Leadership," and Chapter 9, "Do you know yourself")

Most people will know very quickly how you look at the world of work and most importantly how you look at them. But it is important to reinforce your roots, your core values and beliefs, with them at every opportunity. You do this by your actions with and for them, and by what you say and do.

WLLF - Walk, Listen, Learn, Follow-up

Tom Peters, in his many excellent books, emphasizes again and again the importance of getting out in the trenches and **being with** your team members (Management By Wandering Around, MBWA). I will discuss my perspective of this important concept in the next chapter. Keep in mind, however, that getting out and being with your people and being willing to listen to what is important to them is one of the best ways to reinforce who you are and what is important. AND you don't actually have to have a meeting or get on a podium to do it. People will recognize the effort is aimed at and for them. Most of the time you do not even have to say much – walk, listen, learn, follow-up.

Over-the Top-Communication

Communication on every level affords you the opportunity to further your personal agenda (as well as your business agenda). Part of your personal agenda is who you are and what is important to you. Another important part is acknowledging who they are and what is important to them, because that sets the stage for getting things done and getting them done well.

Motivation and inspiration only rarely come from 'Hoo-Hah' speeches. You motivate and inspire by how you treat people, how you listen to them, how you communicate with them on their terms.

Over-the-top communication means paying attention to what you say, how you say it, and most importantly how the people feel about it. If you practice paying attention, really listening and observing, you will learn very quickly what matters most to your team members. And paying attention to people makes them feel important and cared for.

[For more specifics on 'Over-the-top' communications, see Chapter 9 and for "Communicating in Difficult Situations," Chapter 20]

Appreciation, Acknowledgment, Recognition

In other words, show you care on a regular basis. It is not just about evaluations and rewards, it is about the day-to-day, 'Great job on the Bonnard contract Betsy," or "Thanks for getting to that Fibroni project so quickly, Carl. It has made all the difference in the world to the team schedule." [See Chapter 17, "Taking Care of Your People," for a lot of great ideas]

Say what you Mean; Mean what you say

People recognize sincerity; they also recognize insincerity, very readily.

Learn to Communicate without Negativity

There are ALWAYS ways to couch things in terms that are more positive, even difficult messages. [See Chapter 19 "Communicating with Difficult Employees"].

> Author's Note: One of the things I am often asked in executive coaching sessions is "How to say something to someone." It does take practice, but you can learn to temper even difficult remarks so that they are understanding, supportive, and dare I use the word – caring.

What are you saying?

Are you listening carefully to what you say? Have you chosen your words and meaning carefully?

What are you doing?

Actions do speak far louder than words. Expect everything you do to be observed and discussed by your team members.

How does what you say impact others?

Perceptions are everything in a work environment. Everything!

How do the decisions you make and the things you do affect your team?

You will only know if you get out there and listen. Don't talk – just listen, openly and without judgment.

Do you really Care?

They will know. So get yourself straight with this first. This is not something you can hide behind smiles and glad-handing. You really have to have a sense of, "These are MY people."

Ten-twenty-forty-fifty years from now – how many of them will remember?

What will they say about you when you leave the company? THAT is your legacy.

Questions and Ideas for Contemplation

Here is an even tougher question – how many of the people you worked with throughout your life will come to your viewing/funeral?

Leave a legacy of caring behind you – people will remember.

Chapter 6

Walk, Listen, Learn, Follow-Up

Anyone who writes in the business field today is indebted to Tom Peters for 'shouting at the top of his lungs' about many important leadership issues. MBWA - Management By Wandering/Walking Around (with Nancy Austin, *A Passion for Excellence*) put into words something I had slowly discovered through my own trials and tribulations in learning to manage and lead. It is one of the most important techniques I recommend in this book and it is a key to creating the best possible team/people environment so that difficulties between people are far fewer to deal with. This chapter is my slant on this important concept and skill.

Peters and Austin's terminology is catching and a great introduction to a top management skill. I titled this chapter **Walk, Listen, Learn, Follow-up** or **WLLF** because it helps define and remind us of the process. Whatever perspective you use, the important concept is that managers need to get out of their ivory towers/offices and into the trenches to meet and listen to people on their own ground.

You can't know unless you get OUT THERE!

First and foremost getting Out There does **not** mean:

> Holding meetings
>
> Town Hall meetings (which can be a valuable means of listening, but it is not MBWA or WLLF)
>
> One-on-ones in your office – or anyone's office for that matter
>
> Any planned meeting of any kind
>
> It is definitely NOT going to team members' offices and asking questions, e.g.

"Alice, how is the Johnston contract coming along?"

"Bob, do you have the data for the new acquisition yet?"

It is not doing lunch, having a pizza party, or celebrating someone's birthday.

It is not just walking around smiling and glad-handing, either.

These may all be legitimate means of communicating with your employees, but they are not WLLF - Walking, Listening, Learning, and Following-Up. They don't get at the heart of what you are trying to get at which is establishing a trusting, caring relationship with your people.

Walk

You have to get out of your space and into their space. Your space is synonymous with authority, power, formality, decision-making, and level. Keep this important point in mind whenever you are dealing with others. Sometimes it IS important to have these 'accoutrements' as a means of reminding people that there are distinctions in level and authority in the business world. However, when you really want to get to the heart of your business team, your space can be very imposing and it may serve to shut down open and honest communications at a grass roots level.

Their space consists of the corridors and offices/cubicles where they do their jobs, as well as break-rooms and other gathering places. However, and this is a key point, you are not calling a meeting or a gathering, this only really works if it is spontaneous, i.e. you walk into the break room, several people are there, and you start to chat with them.

It really means just taking a half hour or hour once or twice a week (or more, if you can swing it) and walking around touching base with people where they work. The critical thing is how you actually approach this.

Listening

Walking about, once you have a critical perspective of what this means, is the easy part. The hard part is keeping yourself out of the picture and letting everyone else say what they need or want to say. It can take some time to develop the ambiance and trust necessary for this to really work, especially if you have not done this before, or have kept everything fairly formal between you and your employees. Be patient.

Start by selecting a time – it does not always have to be the same time, but people do get used to and often appreciate routine – it is less disruptive. Then walk around and say "Hi"; pop your head into a cubicle or office.

Ask leading questions that are non-specific,

> "How are things going?"
>
> "How's the wife/new baby/dog?"
>
> "Anything I can help you with, Tom?"
>
> "Have any questions I can help you with?"
>
> And so on

Avoid asking any specific questions about work. You can hold other meetings for that. However, you can answer questions directly related to anything someone brings up. Always keep in mind that this is their opportunity to say anything they want to say to you or ask you about anything on their minds, work related or not. Try not to jump on a bandwagon in answering a question. This is you getting to know their needs, wants, and desires.

Be open and, very importantly, supportive of their willingness to speak with you. Respond kindly and intelligently, but don't pass any judgments on what you are offered unless specifically asked. Even then it is probably best to defer them to a time when you can have a more formal meeting.

> "Some good questions, Bob, and I have some ideas. I want to talk with Alice and Jeff about these before making any decisions. Maybe we should meet about this soon. I will work on it. Be sure to kick me into gear if you don't hear from me by the end of the week."

Encourage people to talk

Use good basic communication techniques to help people open up:

Nod; Say "Uh-huh," "Yup," "I see...," whatever is comfortable for you and keeps them going.

Also, things like, "I see," "Great idea," "That's an interesting take, John," and so on

Use similar phraseology to keep them going.

Let them talk – some people may take an indirect route to what they really want to talk about. Don't jump in right away if there is a pregnant pause. You may be surprised at what people will come out with if you give them the leeway and the time to get to the heart of their concerns and wishes.

Don't change the conversation; let them. Listen to whatever they want/need to talk about.

When appropriate, without being obsequious or over-the-top, acknowledge them and show appreciation to them for sharing with you.

Show you are listening:

> Focus on them
>
> Respond to their statements, questions
>
> Paraphrase back things they have said
>
> Sum up your understanding of what they are trying to get across

Say "Thanks," a lot.

Keep a notepad with you and take notes of things people want you to get back to them about.

Don't get frustrated if time after time all they say is, "I'm cool, Joe. No, problems." Keep the door open with a statement like, "Remember I am here for you, Bret. Just let me know if you have any concerns."

Above all be patient – it will take time for people to understand what you are trying to do, that you are open to anything they want to say, that you will listen without judgment, and that you are sincere.

Don't pass judgments!

It can be very difficult to develop the skill to avoid judgment-making statements, but it is critical to helping people reach a point where they will open up and trust the process you are trying to develop – which is open, honest dialogue.

Watch what you say and how you say it. 'Buts...' are qualifications of someone else's ideas, e.g. "Steve, I like what you're saying, but..."

It is so easy to do this, and we don't realize until they suddenly clam up, that we have made a judgment or qualified their statement.

Listen carefully to what they say and make your best on-the-spot interpretation of what needs to follow. It is not that you can't say what is on your mind. Your aim, however, is to open things up, not shut them down. Keep in mind that how we say things can either facilitate openness or close doors. By self-observation and by observing the reactions of others, you can learn to communicate openly without shutting others down.

Keep it light

Respond in an appropriate manner to what others say to you but in general, as you do your walk-about, keep everything on a friendly, easy-going basis. You are not checking on people to see whether they are accomplishing things. You are not out there to see how many people are gathered around the water cooler.

> Which is another reason that a set time for this can be better than a spontaneous decision to just roam the halls – they won't get nervous when you suddenly appear. Plus in the long run they will anticipate actually having some quality time with you. You are there to take the pulse on how your team feels, and about what is important to them.
>
> Spontaneous, unannounced walking the halls can also work IF they are used to this process, i.e. they know that formal meetings are for formal discussions, and when you are out and about, anything goes.

Learn

There are many things you can learn from this process:

What is on their minds

What is important to them – the things that really matter

A bit about who they are, their lives outside of work, etc.

A good deal about quality management and leadership if you keep your ears open

An amazing number of ideas: good, bad, and indifferent and likely some great ones

The ebb and flow of office politics and intrigue – you won't get it all, but you will start to see what the waters are like

Who they are – as people, not just as employees

And, if you really pay attention, a good bit about life

Over time this process can help you a great deal with your own growth as a person, a manager, and as a leader of people. Not only will you find that your team members are more open, productive, and quality-minded; you will find that they care. You will also find that you have far fewer concerns to deal with on an interpersonal level, and far fewer communication problems throughout your part of the organization.

Pay attention to what your people are telling you and to what is important to them, and you will learn how to best deal with concerns that do arise. You and your team will be more able to weather changes and difficulties that come from without as well.

Really dedicating yourself to WLLF – Walking, Listening, Learning, and Follow-up – will help you lessen your own stress, and believe it or not, your time commitment. Because even though you are dedicating X amount of time to the process, you will have far fewer concerns coming to your door on a daily basis.

Follow-up

Even with the best intentions, great communication skills, and sincerity this process will only work if you are willing to follow-through with questions and concerns that arise. Do this as quickly as possible. Ideally, as soon as you get back to your office, fire off some e-mails to people thanking them for their openness and willingness to share. Then deal immediately with everything that was brought up that you reasonably can in the next fifteen minutes.

If there are issues that will take longer, send a quick e-mail to the person(s) who brought the concern forward letting them know you paid attention and that you are on top of it. Then remember to follow-up after that.

Remember – people talk about things that are important to them no matter how trivial it may seem to you. Let them know that what they care about matters.

You don't have to accomplish everything they ask you to do. You don't always have to have an answer. You do have to try, look in to it, make some kind of effort to understand and look for solutions. You also have to get back to them and offer an explanation as to why what they proposed, what they were concerned about, etc., is or is not feasible.

I really can't afford the time

You really cannot afford NOT to make the time because this may be the single most important means you have for avoiding a ton of difficulties in the workplace and for motivating your team members.

But...

'Buts' are excuses...Do you want your leadership quality to be based fundamentally around excuses?

Even if you are the manager of several teams – which are led by managers of other teams who have many reports, getting into the trenches on a regular basis says a ton about who you are...

> as a person

> as a manager

> and as a leader.

As simple as this may seem on the surface, it is anything but to the people who see you and get to talk with you.

Just Do it

You will be glad you did, especially when you see the results. Plus, you will feel better about yourself – funny thing that, but it does work.

Questions and Ideas for Contemplation

Author's Note: I have been shouting this, sometimes literally, to my executive clients, too. Unfortunately, the 'I'm too busy sign,' keeps flashing for many of them (See next two chapters: "Bureaucracy" and "Time Management"). You have to be willing to commit yourself to this just as you would commit yourself to a weekly high level meeting. When you do, you will experience remarkable results. If you don't, well, work does go on.

Make a commitment to yourself and schedule some time each week for several months to get out there and

Walk, Listen, Learn, and Follow-Up. You will find that the time is worth it and your schedule will not be any the worse for having done so. It may even suddenly seem like things have lightened up considerably.

Chapter 7

Bureaucracy

One of the main causes of problems in the workplace seems to come from the constraints and demands placed on us by them – 'them' being the organization, the higher-ups, upper management, Human Resources, legal departments, etc. These concerns equate to a good bit of stress and tension, and in today's business world, serious problems with time management (see next chapter).

Is there a way around, over, through bureaucratic nonsense?

Can you deal with all of these roadblocks and still succeed at job as not only a manager, but as a leader – a leader who cares enough to make a difference with people?

The Problems

Do these sound familiar?

Too many meetings

Too much irrelevant busy-work you have to do

Too many forms

Too many layers

Too many 'have-tas'

"Human Resources says I haveta take this course."

"The boss says we haveta do this a certain way."

"I haveta do this off-site Tuesday and Wednesday; no time for the troops."

"I haveta have this in by Monday."

Not enough time despite working 12 hour days, nights, and the 'occasional' weekend.

And a myriad of other things

The Solution

YOU are the only solution!

You can blame, point your finger in any direction you want, complain, whine, groan and moan, and work yourself, literally, to death, but you won't accomplish an easing of these types of problems unless you are willing to accept responsibility for the problem – which will give you the power and control to find solutions.

The basic dilemma is that we accept these things and too often are unwilling to raise our voices enough to make (insist on) changes.

"But she's my boss. I can't tell her, I'm too busy."

"This off site is the pet project of the senior vice president of research. Even though it isn't directly related to my team, I better go."

Bureaucracy lives on because often we tend to let it live on. We live with it, rather than finding better ways to do things. We accept dicta, instead of offering alternatives. We say 'Yes,' when we could say,

"Maybe"

"No"

"What about..."

"I think there might be a better way."

"Have you considered..."

"I think we could probably get this done in forty-five minutes." (Instead of that one or two hour meeting)

Author's Note: In working with executives as a coach I discovered early on that once a manager feels overwhelmed by their work situation – which IS the most common scenario today in the business world -- they are less inclined to seek other solutions, because they have been drained of energy. They don't have the time or inclination for out-of-the-box thinking.

Once they commit to taking the bull by the horns and instigating change and creating opportunities, their work lives can change dramatically for the better, both frustration-wise and time-wise – less stress, less tension, fewer long days, nights, and weekends. It all starts with accepting personal responsibility for one's plight. You may be **right** to complain and blame others for your work constraints, but it isn't going to change anything.

[Note: Good coaches open doors; they don't solve executives' problems. They empower the executives to find their own solutions.]

It does take personal commitment and courage. You have to be willing to effect change by accepting that things can change if you are willing to push back. Very often there are positive ways to make things happen without stepping on anyone's toes. You do have to be intelligent, judicious, willing to stick your neck out occasionally, and be willing to take responsibility for all of your actions, suggestions, and plans. And you have to be patient because change does take time.

You also may have to persevere when you are trying to get others to buy into your ideas.

Ownership, Power, and Control

Bureaucracy lives within the framework of who has the power and control in any given situation. You may believe that this is the sole domain of 'the powers that be.' It is important to keep in mind that real power and control are within yourself (see Chapter 13). When you can allow someone else to maintain the illusion of having all the power and control, you have a much better chance of changing things (and their mind).

There are many ways to approach change, but the best chance of success is to couch your ideas in terms that allow the other person ownership in the change, ownership of the new solution, i.e. some of or all of the illusion of having the power and control.

> "John, we have been talking around the issue of cutting back on some of the forms and levels of sign-offs for some time, I think you have some great ideas on this. One thing you mentioned awhile back got me to thinking and I have designed a package based around what you said. Take a look at this and see what you think."

If John is rigid about keeping control, you have given him at least partial ownership of your solution. It really does not cost you anything and it may just bring him on board – at least enough to start listening. He will probably still want his finger in the pie, and he may make a ton of suggestions and changes, but you have given direction to a positive solution to a major concern that he may very well now buy into; which perhaps before, he was reluctant to even consider.

Author's Note: I have rarely run into a bureaucratic roadblock that did not have a way around it or that could not be improved with an intelligent and creative approach. It can take time, energy, and perseverance, but the end result may very well make your life and the lives of others/your team members, considerably easier.

Recognize power and control

Change and the acceptance of new ideas is much easier when you set the stage by paying attention to people. You do this by appreciation, acknowledgment, empowerment, and recognition. AND, this is not just something you should do with the powers that be. Practice it with everyone and you won't appear obsequious; it will just be the kind of person you are.

Appreciation

Everyone likes to be appreciated. Letting them (employees, your boss, colleagues, etc.) know that you appreciate even the small things they do for you sets the stage for them listening to the big things you want to do. From the custodial staff to top management, from your administrative assistant to Human Resources, and with everyone else you contact every day, appreciation makes a major difference. Be sincere and let them know by every means you have available – quick e-mails, a personal phone call, a pat on the back in the hallway, a formal letter, etc.

Acknowledgment

Sometimes all it takes is letting people know that you know how important they are to you and your team. Acknowledgment and

Appreciation go hand in hand. WLLF – Walk, Listen, Learn, Follow-up (or WBWA – Management By Wandering Around – Peters and Austin) is one of the best ways to acknowledge an individual or a team. Instead of sending that e-mail, go over and spend five minutes with them just chatting. Over time it works wonders.

Empowerment

Appreciate and Acknowledgment help empower people. Listening is the best form of empowerment there is. Listening, understanding, and thanking someone for their input and their ideas helps create a receptive environment for your own ideas. Hint: This will work with your boss, too!

Recognition

Recognition and reward let people know you think they are special. Used judiciously, recognizing someone for something they have done for you/your team, can open doors that might otherwise remain forever closed.

Make an effort to occasionally recognize your boss, especially when he/she has opened some doors for you. It will help to reinfore behaviors you want to see.

[There will be more on these important concepts throughout this book; see specifically Chapter 17. "Taking Care of Your People."]

There's the wall – what are you going to do?

There are always blocks created by years and layers of bureaucracy. You do have choices you can make. You can continually beat your head into the wall – or you can empower yourself through intelligent, creative, and positive changes that make a difference. It is about what kind of leader you want to be – one with personal power and personal control who finds ways to appreciate and empower others – or something else.

Take a Chance

Steve Brodie did, and he built his life around it.

In Memoriam Charlie Leonhard (Dr. Charles Leonhard)

My major Doctoral advisor often told the story of Steve Brodie, the first and only person to jump off the Brooklyn Bridge and live. He did not recommend that we try mimicking the stunt; he was trying to inspire us to take chances. I will always remember the way he told the story because he had so much fun telling it. He never offered any explanation, but there was always a twinkle in his eye as he exhorted us to ever higher heights in our work. One day I felt impelled to check out what actually happened.

The truth is, more likely, that Steve Brodie didn't jump. It is believed that a dummy was thrown off the bridge instead and a boat picked Steve out of the water as if he had jumped. In any case, Steve made enough of a sensation from the 'leap' that he starred in a play that featured a reenactment of the 'event, and subsequently opened a popular bar.

Taking chances is not about unwisely jumping off of high bridges or into shark-filled waters. It is about using your intelligence and wisdom to make a difference for you and for your team.

Questions and Ideas for Contemplation

There is almost always an opportunity in that bureaucratic challenge you are facing. It may not be obvious, and it may mean you have to go up against some serious ingrained opposition. Seek out and take on the challenges that will help you make a difference.

Chapter 8

Time Management

Bureaucracy and Time Management concerns are two sides of the same coin.

Can you make a Difference?

Reiterating a key point – YOU are the only solution! You have to accept responsibility for the problem before you will ever find a long term solution.

The problem is you don't have enough time to accomplish everything because of:

>Your boss

>Other department demands (Human Resources, etc.)

>Too many meetings – too long, boring, irrelevant

>Too many e-mails – too long, too rambling, too irrelevant

>Too many forms, memos, requisitions, etc.

>Matrix and Line demands

>Employee demands

>Coworker demands

>Bureaucracy

>'Them'

>And so on.

Time management is a seminar by itself, but the real key for success is **self-empowerment** – your willingness to step up to the plate, take responsibility on your own shoulders, and to make changes. Here are some great ideas to get you started:

Structure

Structure is about the parameters we set or are willing to accept.

As a leader of a team, we have the responsibility to ourselves and to our players to set parameters for what is acceptable and what is not. Far too often we leave these things to chance.

> Do you have specific parameters for how meetings are held, timed, organized/planned, led/run, prepared for?
>
> For e-mails? Length, content, focus, attachments, etc.
>
> Papers, forms, publications, presentations, etc.
>
> Time tables – too often we let deadlines slide. Keep to your own deadlines, and make sure everyone on your team (and in the line and matrix) understand that you expect them to stick to deadlines as well.
>
> And so on.

Keep in mind that parameters are guides, not rigid sets of rules. I firmly believe in creativity and new ideas. However, suggested and intelligent ways to handle some of the many things we and our team members do on a regular basis can help guide everyone to better time usage.

Hint: The wise leader is open at all times for ideas that may be even better than what he/she may have recommended.

A quick example:

> If you really want team meetings (any meetings you or your team are involved in) to run smoothly, efficiently, and on time, set some parameters for meeting preparation:
>
>> A detailed agenda available 'x' amount of time ahead of meeting
>>
>> Everyone is expected to read the agenda ahead of time
>>
>> Data should be prepared and ready to hand out or disseminated ahead of time
>>
>> Everyone is expected to come prepared
>>
>> And so on

Structure does not have to be limiting. It can leave some doors wide open, but it does say that 'this' and 'this' are important considerations and that "We can all be better at what we do if we do 'X'."

You also have to be committed to making sure everyone is on board with these guidelines and makes an effort to implement them. Letting things slide can quickly create a non-compliant attitude and a fall back into old habits.

Structure and 'difficult' people/difficult situations

A certain amount of structure gives people something they can fall back on when things are difficult. The stresses of ongoing change in today's business climate can be partially minimized by setting some solid guidelines for people to rely on when the going gets tough.

Structure can also give team members ideals to work toward and even offer opportunities for recognition and reward for success.

Is that meeting really necessary?

Meetings, committees, extra teams, etc., are often more time intensive than other means of approaching a concern. Find the best solution – not 'the usual solution,' i.e. scheduling another meeting. Forming a committee or scheduling a meeting to discuss something may be the worst possible use of everyone's time. Think it through! Don't do something out of habit. Too often we charge ahead without really planning:

> "Marge, let's have a meeting on the Brook deal from three to five tomorrow."

> The truth may be that the only reason for the meeting is to get Sally and Dave on board. Maybe a phone call to Sally and dropping into Dave's office on your way to lunch will work just as well, and you will save you and your two team members an hour and a half or more of time each.

Set the **time** for a meeting based on what needs to be accomplished, not "Let's meet for an hour every Wednesday." There is nothing sacred about one hour or two hour meetings, especially if you can get the work accomplished in twenty minutes.

> Hint: setting clear, focused agendas can help expedite meeting times many-fold.

We all tend to fall into the trap of setting meeting times to convenient blocks of half hours, hours, two hours etc. When we actually choose a time based on a specific agenda and then make the effort to stick to it, we can typically get much more accomplished in shorter time blocks.

Make a commitment to challenge yourself and your team to schedule meetings with tight agendas that you plan to stick to. Try to get away from locking into an hour or a half hour. If fifteen or twenty minutes will do, then schedule that way.

Interestingly, if we set a meeting time to a shorter time span we, and the people who come to the meeting, are more likely to make an effort to get done in the required time (or nearly the required time!). And the converse is true. If we set a meeting for two hours, it WILL take two hours **and more** to get through the agenda, even if we legitimately could have done it in an hour and twenty minutes.

Manage meetings – both the ones you run and the ones other people run.

There are ways to keep people on track and to bring them back to focus when they get off track. In essence you have to be a bit stubborn about maintaining focus. Help train your personnel to maintain focus as well.

You should have two key priorities:

> Anything that DIRECTLY affects or impacts your vision (values, goals, mission).

> Your people

Everything else is secondary – act and schedule accordingly

When things get off track, refocus.

> Author's Note: A key technique I have used a thousand times (and it only feels awkward the first couple of times you use it) is to raise your hand. I have even used this successfully many times in meetings with my bosses and their bosses. Raise your hand (which is one sure way to

get a word in) and help the meeting refocus,

> "This is great discussion, but I know we all have something scheduled after this. I was wondering if we could have a vote on the proposed amendment to the contract and move on to the next point."

I called for many a vote in my day!

No one wants to get far off track and to waste time. People have busy schedules and they want to get done and out the door. You can help, whether you are leading the meeting or just another cog in the wheel. This is YOUR time someone is taking up. Take responsibility and be willing to stick your neck out if you need to. Ninety-nine times out of a hundred everyone in the room will appreciate it – they just didn't have the chutzpah that you do to kick things back into gear.

WLLF – Walk, Listen, Learn, Follow-up

Walking around and having your fingers on the pulse of your team can save you a lot of time that might otherwise be spent in group meetings and one-on-ones trying to figure out what is going on or what went wrong. It is about keeping on top of things and getting to important issues before they become critical issues.

Little blocks of time

I have used this technique since my doctoral days when I used to always have notes, a book, or a tape with me wherever I went. I studied in cars/buses, in lines, waiting on the phone for someone 'to get back to me,' walking from here to there, and walking from there to here. I used as many of those little blocks of time as I could because I had a wife and small child at home that I wanted to spend some quality time with. I actually very rarely had to set aside extra time to study. Sometimes all I got in on one of these 'breaks' was to study one formula for statistics classes. At other times, the long walks between classes afforded me time to read and underline a whole chapter in a book.

Today we have PDAs and cell phones, but there are still lots of little blocks of time you probably don't use where electronics might not be appropriate. It is not so much multitasking as being prepared ahead of time to make use of the time we might be waiting for something else to happen...or getting from here to there, or there to here.

Set an Example

Set an example of time management for your troops. Better yet, let people know how you expect things to be done (structure) and be sure you follow your own recommendations.

E-mail

Everyone wastes far too many hours a day on e-mails. Setting parameters (guidelines – not rules) for business e-mails can save everyone time. A semi-formal structure can make them easier to write and to read, plus everyone knows what to expect.

Key hints:

> Keep them short. The majority of e-mails should be less than a computer screen in length and someone should be able to read them in less than two minutes (preferably less than a minute). Any longer than this and we tend to set the e-mail aside for later reading. IF that occurs, it is probably at twelve-thirty in the morning when we are desperately hoping to get to bed within the next couple of hours.
>
> One main or key idea per e-mail; anything more and people begin to lose interest
>
> Unless inappropriate, use outline form; it is easy to read, easy to focus on points, and helps keep things terse
>
> Attach any supporting materials; if it is in the body of the e-mail people will likely table the e-mail until later. You probably know what happens to a majority of those e-mails!

Expect the best

Don't accept anything less: a great amount of time is wasted in the business world because managers let deadlines slide, let people get away with coming unprepared to meetings, let their team members come in late, etc. Let them know what you expect; insist on quality; insist on **on-time quality**! You set the stage. How do you CHOOSE to set it today? Tomorrow? This IS your work-life.

Don't be afraid to delegate

It gives responsibility and the opportunity for growth to team members and it saves you time and energy. Some of your greatest resources for time management are your best performers – those who have the potential for growth and advancement. Trust your team members to do their best and they will very often step to the plate and help out. It takes things off your plate and in addition helps build your team. It also gives you more opportunities to appreciate and acknowledge team members for the work they do.

Your personal time-management efforts can affect everyone. They can even begin to have an influence up the line. People notice when positive things happen.

Questions and Ideas for Contemplation

Taking personal responsibility for bureaucracy and time management is a major leap for most executives. When you can make that leap, you empower yourself and your team to make a difference. Change higher up the line may take some time, but it can happen if you persevere and go about things the right way. Keep in mind that everything you do and say at work has an impact – make that work for you.

Be an exemplar of time management. When you find something that helps/works, let your team members know. Have others share their ideas with you and the team as well.

Chapter 9

Keys to Boss – Employee Communications

Set an Example

Many concerns in the workplace, particularly relationship concerns, are caused by poor and disruptive communication between coworkers, employees and their bosses, and most certainly between bosses and their employees. You have the power to affect all communication within your purview – choose wisely.

Biggest communication problem for managers?

Under-communicating!

People like to be kept informed. They like to understand. They want to be 'in the know.' In the hectic world of business, it is best to assume that far too much that is important is slipping through the cracks. That is why I emphasize over-communicating. Use every resource and tool you have available to get the word out. Then it is often wise to do it again. When something is important, it is almost essential to do it again, i.e. to follow-up a communiqué, whatever the form, with some form of reminder.

The better informed everyone is, including all your team members and everyone they connect with on a daily basis, the fewer problems you will have as a manager and as a leader. You can't just expect everyone to open up and be forthright and honest; you have to create the space and atmosphere which allows that to blossom.

Say it!

Many managers don't put into words things that need to be communicated. They somehow assume that all of this information and understanding will leak out – it may, but you really don't want to know in what form some of it does.

There is an old saying that gets partially to the heart of this – "Say what you Mean and Mean what you Say." However, you should also consider how these phrases further delineate what needs to happen in your work space:

Say what you are thinking

People can't read your mind and lest they misinterpret something, it is wise to get in the habit of stating or putting down on paper (or both), information and ideas that you feel are important. You may think you do this. The truth is most of us rarely do it enough. You have to pay attention to yourself and practice this skill.

Say who you are and what is important to you

Yes, people will understand some things about you by your actions, but saying it out loud and frequently reinforces, and in some cases over-emphasizes, things that need to be over-emphasized. For example:

> You may believe in honesty and try to present yourself as an open and honest leader. However, actually stating this frequently drives the point home.

>> "Alyce, I appreciate your honesty. Openness is one of the keys to effective communications. Keep it up."

There will be no doubt about how you feel about subterfuge and backhanded tactics, so if they occur, you have a foundation upon which to deal with them. And you will not only set an example, you will live it in thoughts, words, and deeds.

Create openness by being open

A recurrent problem with managers is that they tend to hold some things close to the chest. People like to be kept informed, and to the extent you can keep them informed, it is wise to do so. Sometimes it is wise to do it with a bit of fanfare.

Another related concern that is very prevalent in business is the manager who clams up when he/she has been told not to divulge certain pieces of information. Everyone knows that there is often privileged information at work. What many people don't know is that it is important to state that fact to your employees, particularly if there are questions and rumors afoot that may affect their work and lives.

Say it: "I know you are all anxious about the changes that have been announced. I am currently involved in strategy meetings, but I am not at liberty to tell you much at this stage. I will let you know, as soon as it is appropriate to do so, everything I can. Please bear with me as we make the most of this difficult situation for all."

Then keep following this up regularly with everything you can to help them understand what is happening. Whatever news you share is better than nothing, and far better than rumors.

Say what needs to be said

Sometimes managers simply avoid passing on unpleasant news. This can be very frustrating to everyone involved and can even be devastating to the morale of your team. It is often far worse to delay bad news, as worrying and rumors will likely set in. Make it a habit to be willing to deal with something unpleasant immediately.

There are always ways to temper difficult and unpleasant communication and to say things in a supportive, kind manner. It does take practice and if you feel some angst about your ability in this arena, get a good coach. They are trained to facilitate communications and can help you build your skills.

Get to the bottom of concerns NOW!

Rumors, interpersonal difficulties, and negative behaviors don't just go away if you ignore them. Getting people talking and opening up about concerns they have are the most important steps toward finding resolutions to problems. The sooner you deal with difficulties, the easier it will be to find solutions.

Put it in writing

Important information needs to be documented and reinforced. The best way to do this is through written communications. Remember that you set the stage for the ease and significance of the electronic information that flows between members of your team. Delineate guidelines that give everyone a clear heads up when important information is being presented.

Use both verbal **and** written information-sharing whenever possible to emphasize key ideas, important information, and to show appreciation, acknowledgment, etc. If they don't get it one way, hopefully they will get it the other, and it never hurts for them to hear it more than once. Many difficulties arise in the work place because managers assume that people get something even though they have made no real effort to communicate their ideas, values, intent, etc. and/or they don't communicate enough. Repetition works: it reinforces what has already been offered; it helps emphasize important ideas; it helps make sure everyone got it; and it helps to remind everyone.

Be honest (see Chapter 14)

There is no room, ever, for dissembling at work. If it is part of the culture, then you may want to make an effort to change the culture within your purview or look for another job. Nothing good comes from evasiveness or dishonesty in the workplace. If you want your team members to be open and honest with you, you will need to be open and honest with them.

Say it again

Don't get too complacent about how great a communicator you are. Most of us can use frequent self-reminders that we need to keep our communications over-the-top. That means making sure everyone got it and got it right. Important things should be said more than once and through as many different venues as possible.

When in doubt ASK!

Asking is one of the single most important communication tools we have, and we use it far too infrequently.

> Asking denotes concern, shows a willingness to understand, and offers respect and acknowledgment

> It also promotes learning, for you and others.

> It is almost always a win-win-win technique – **IF** we are open and non-judgmental about the answers we get.

Avoid judgments, especially when listening to others

This does not mean you can't disagree with people. It means you need to give them the opportunity and space to say what they want and need to say. Then you need to consider what they have related to you very carefully. Spend a bit of time developing a supportive, kind response. If you don't do this, people will clam up and you will have managed yourself into a corner when it comes to communicating with team members. Creativity and motivation will be out the window as well.

Temper your communications and directives with support, encouragement, and appreciation. These go a long way to keeping key lines open for continued sharing. If you need to spend fifteen minutes hashing through data or a report with someone, throw some kudos in the mix.

Get in the habit of offering people something positive every time you talk with them:

> "I like the way you think, Annie. Keep the ideas flowing."

> "Keep up the good work, Bob. I like your doggedness. The project is looking great."

> "Thanks for the input, Sally. Keeping on top of things helps us avoid mistakes."

> "Hey, Nathan. Thanks! That means a lot to me. I appreciate the feedback."

> "That's very insightful, Pete. I hadn't thought of it that way at all. Give me some time to mull this over. I'm not sure we can use it yet, but I like how you are looking for other takes on this problem."

Perceptions **are** everything. Believe it or not:

It doesn't matter what you meant if they don't get it;

it matters how someone takes it.

Observe not only your own communications, but pay attention to how others **take** what you say. If you are not getting important ideas across the way you want, find out why, and then work on your skills and techniques. Don't assume that because you said it that they got it.

> Make sure your meaning is clear
>
> Learn to use repetition effectively
>
> Be willing to ask if they understand, if they 'got it'
>
> Use of a variety of venues – memo, e-mail, in-person, meetings
>
> Listen carefully to their response

In other words over-communicate whenever you want to be sure someone gets the message.

Directing versus Empowerment

As a boss/authority figure you do have the power to direct people and to order them around. Some managers only understand this method of dealing with subordinates. It may get the job done, but at what cost?

> To your team?
>
> To individuals?
>
> To yourself?

Empowering people creates a different office atmosphere – it is motivational, encourages creativity, helps people feel unique and appreciated, and often saves time, energy, and money on your part as well as theirs.

Yes, you can control people, but keep in mind that the only true form of control is self-control. (See Chapter 13)

Being more supportive and empowering, and as a result less directive, is all about how you say things, how you do things, and how people interpret your words and actions.

Most importantly

Every time you are with another person at work you have the opportunity to leave them with a positive feeling...or something else.

Remember they are 'your people' – choose wisely.

Questions and Ideas for Contemplation

The proof of your communications is in the results you get. Observe, make adjustments, practice, gain new skills. Use a coach or mentor if there are areas in which you feel you could beef up your abilities. It will be well worth the time, energy, and money.

We will discuss these Key communication skills and techniques throughout the rest of this book. Many times learning IS about repetition!

Chapter 10

Self-Awareness

Gnothi Seauton
Know Yourself

Inscribed above the entrance at the Temple of Apollo at Delphi

(Attributed to Socrates, Solon, et al)

How well do you know yourself?

The Seven Keys to Understanding and Working with Difficult People

Self-Awareness

Self-worth

Self-Confidence

Self-Control

Honesty

Kindness

Positivity

These Seven Keys were derived from extensive research and experience in the field of "Understanding and Working with Difficult People." In the next seven chapters these key ideas will be discussed relevant to a manager's perspective in dealing with difficult employees. For an annotated broad outline of "The Seven Keys" as they relate to "Understanding and Working with Difficult People," see Appendix I at the end of this book.

Self-Awareness

We all like to think we know ourselves quite well. The truth, if we are honest with ourselves, is that self-understanding is a long growth process that continues throughout our lives. By simply looking back at our teenage years or our early adult years, we can understand this perspective.

Self-awareness takes extensive practice paying attention to:

> What we say
>
> What we do
>
> How we think and what we think about
>
> Our emotions and reactions
>
> How we come across to others
>
> Paying attention to our values – keeping these to the forefront of our personal work as we support and interact with others

What we Say; How we Say it

You can learn a good bit about yourself by paying close attention to your communications. Add to this, paying attention to how people react to what you say and how you say it, and you will begin to acquire some very useful managerial and leadership skills.

It is useful to spend a week or two conscientiously watching yourself and your communications with others. Take mental notes of what seems to work best and what doesn't. Do this once every six months, or simply get in the habit of checking on yourself. When we are on top of what we say and how we say it – including vocal tone, gestures, posture, and facial expressions as well as the meaning and intent of what we say – we can develop an amazing amount of control.

What we think about, and How we think

What we spend time on in our own minds is reflected in everything we do – our words, our actions, our written communications, our gestures and facial expressions, how we move, walk, etc. People can read these cues quite well. While we may aim at being an out-going, open, upbeat, caring professional, if we spend a good bit of time worrying, thinking negatively, and so on, it will show and it will impact others.

Who you are as a complete person affects

all the other people you interact with.

Just as you can't leave the office completely in the office when you go home; you can't leave all the other things that impact your life out of the office – especially what is churning around inside you.

Emotions

Stuffing your emotions away so others don't see them may seem like a good tactic, but it is not healthy, for you or for anyone who contacts you in your role as a leader. Paying attention to and trying to understand how you feel helps you deal with things that are of importance to you. When you are more aware of how you feel, you have the opportunity to deal with those feelings. You can do this in a variety of ways:

Admit to yourself what you are feeling in reaction to any situation.

Simply acknowledging how you feel about something helps you begin to deal with it. Pushing it back out of your consciousness creates inner tension that can affect you for a long time, and it will affect others.

Share with trusted others

Talk with your wife, a colleague (at the same level), a coach or mentor. If it is a serious concern, you may want to consider contacting a minister, counselor, or another professional trained in a specific area

Write out your feelings and thoughts

This is a very effective means of working through worries and concerns. Write until you feel you have a solid foundation of understanding and awareness for dealing with the problem. This process can be very cathartic. It also gives you a chance to organize your feelings and thoughts about the problem and thus gives you a beginning framework for finding a solution or getting help.

> Author's Note: I have found the technique of writing down worries or concerns very helpful. I find I am able to get a handle on them more readily and once it is all down on paper or on my computer I seem to relinquish the need to stress about it so much. The process of writing it down seems to get it 'out there' and I am able to release the emotional attachment to the problem somewhat. It becomes much more concrete and workable.

Get some exercise

Work out, take a walk, etc. while you think through the problem

Enlist the aid of team members or colleagues

You can do this by directly asking for their help in relation to a specific concern, or you can raise a generic perspective of the problem in a meeting and let others help 'you' work through the concern. This can be an effective way to deal with work related problems. Getting input from others is a positive way to get team members involved and to give them responsibility and ownership. This is probably not the best venue for personal concerns but it can work remarkably well for business problems. Sometimes the best solutions come from the most unlikely of sources.

Reactions

We react to things because our emotions become involved. Experiences and emotions from the past may affect our current reactions to a difficult situation.

Self-awareness of 'How we typically react" and "How we are about to react" can help us maintain self-control and deal with a concerning situation responsively – we choose how we will respond (in-control) rather than react (out-of-control).

Consider these two choices carefully:

> When we react in a difficult situation we are typically not in control and we 'give over,' in a sense, our power and control to another. Our emotions lead the charge.

When we can step back mentally and emotionally, acknowledging how we feel and what we are thinking, we maintain control and can choose to respond in a constructive and hopefully positive way. We change our personal dynamics and the dynamics of the situation tremendously.

Know how other people affect you

When we pay attention to our reactions and interactions with others we can learn a great deal about ourselves. We are all different, and differences are the most common cause of angst between people. By understanding how we are different from other people and how others' actions and words impact us, we can learn/gain the ability to control ourselves in difficult situations.

How we are perceived by others

Whatever our good intentions are, the bottom line in our interactions with others is how they see and interpret what we do and say. Perceptions ARE everything.

Observing how people react to us is a skill that helps us understand ourselves better. However, if you really want to know, have the courage to ask. You can ask a colleague, a superior, a coach or mentor, and yes, you can even ask your employees.

Be prepared – when you ask, you have to listen without blame, but's, excuses, explanations, or judgments of any kind. Listen, accept, learn, and then be sure to thank them. It can be tough on your ego, but it is a great way to learn a good bit about yourself.

Know your values; Talk about them; Live them

In Chapter 3 we discussed the importance of understanding the core values you hold as a leader. Keeping these key qualities at the fore when you work with others helps inspire you and them to do your best.

> Author's Note: I have my 'short list' laminated and keep it in my wallet. It is a good idea to post these someplace where you will see them every day, too.

Letting people know at every opportunity what is important to you helps keep everyone focused on what is most important. You have to 'Say it' – in meetings, conversations, one-on-ones, etc. For example:

> "I do feel strongly about keeping an open and receptive climate around here, Bob. Thanks for sharing."

> "As you know, quality in everything we do is a key to this team's success. Let's all keep up the great work."

Know your Strengths

You know what you are good at – use those strengths to your advantage.

Understand your Weaknesses

Acknowledge what you don't do as well as you would like. You may have reached a level of management where you are leading teams that are far removed from your key areas of expertise. Don't hide from this 'weakness,' use it to learn, grow, anticipate. Create strength and responsibility in others by using those who do have that unique skill/knowledge set. Be willing to get help and make allowances when you need to.

People respect competence, but they respect honesty just as much, or more.

Self-Knowledge – the key to excellence

Self-awareness is the first of "The Seven Keys to Understanding and Working with Difficult People," because it helps us understand and build the other six.

Questions and Ideas for Contemplation

Challenge yourself through self-observation to understand the many key points discussed above. You will learn a tremendous amount about yourself and about how you affect others.

You may be very surprised at how much you do learn about yourself in a short period of time. Your leadership and people skills will grow with this effort.

Chapter 11

Self-Worth

If you don't feel good about yourself;

it is highly unlikely you will feel good about others.

Self-Worth vs Ego

Self-worth

is

knowing you are a person of value and consequence

and being content with that.

Ego

is

placing yourself above others.

Our egos require constant maintenance, often in the form of building oneself up, and putting others down. Egos are self-protective, defensive, directive, controlling, and uneasy.

How do you feel about yourself?

Ask yourself these questions and spend some time thinking of your answers as well as the deeper meanings these questions connote.

Do you feel confident in the values and qualities you hold close to your heart?

Do you make every effort to live these values as a manager and leader?

Are you comfortable with others having center stage?

Can you have true appreciation and joy for others' accomplishments?

Can you value other people's opinions, ideas, beliefs, and approaches to things even if they are different from your own?

Are you comfortable with delegating responsibility and authority?

Do you feel at ease with others regardless of how they are presenting themselves to you?

Do you take responsibility for your own life and work? For your strengths **and** weaknesses?

Do you feel capable and confident when dealing with people of greater authority than yourself?

Are you willing to stand up for your own ideas and beliefs as well as the ideas and beliefs of your team members when it is called for?

Try posting these questions in your office where you can readily see them and ask yourself them anytime things seem to be getting a bit tough, or when you have a difficult decision to make.

Power

Managers and leaders have power – power to make decisions, power to evaluate, power over others, and so on.

How you use this power is what defines you

as a leader of others.

If you do not think you have power, ask anyone who has been in an authority position for any length of time and then moved on or retired how it feels to step down. There is almost always a sense of loss – of power, control, privileges, etc.

The use or abuse of power is a key factor in whether others willingly follow you into the fray or whether they have to be pushed kicking and screaming. Power can corrupt. A wise leader understands the power he/she wields and tempers what they do and say, the decisions they make, everything they do **by understanding how that power impacts others**.

Personality

A great deal has been written about the personal characteristics of great leaders and about their personalities. The truth about leadership is that if one looks at a wide range of leaders – good, great, and not so great – they are an amazingly diverse group of personalities and leadership types. Great leadership is about the power you have within yourself and how you successfully use that personal power in your work with others.

People recognize personal power in someone, whether they are quiet and reserved or bombastic and energetic. They also recognize the controlled and judicious understanding use of power. Self-worth is about personal power and self-control (see Chapter 12).

How DO you feel about yourself?

Perhaps a universal trait of quality leaders is an underlying self-confidence (see next chapter). People recognize it in the way they carry themselves, in the small everyday things they do, and in the ways they interact with others. You are the only person who can fully understand how you feel about yourself, but you can be assured that others will know how you feel overall.

It is the extremely rare person who grows up in life with no trials or tribulations to mar their confidence. Working through negative feelings we have about who we are and how we approach others is an important means of developing a more positive sense of self. One achieves self-worth through self-awareness.

The Self-Awareness – Self-worth process

The **first step** in this process of self-growth is to recognize when and what types of concerns, interactions, etc. affect you negatively. In other words:

> Do certain types of behaviors irritate or bother you?
>
> Do some types of pressure situations create frustrations that are difficult to deal with?

Are you negatively impacted by some personalities and not others?

And so on.

The more specific you can delineate things that bother you, the better you will understand yourself and be able to deal with them. Self-awareness in this sense helps lead to self-control, self-confidence, and ultimately better self-worth.

The **next step** is to focus on your reactions and feelings to situations or actions that cause you upset – feelings of being out-of-control, worry, etc. When you understand yourself better, you have the power to make other choices. As you develop the skill to step back in difficult situations and pause for an instant to assess what is happening and how you are feeling, you are already developing more personal power. The more you practice this skill the fewer your concerns will be.

The final step is to make better choices for yourself: learn to **respond** to people and situations that impact you negatively; don't lose control/give over your control by reacting negatively.

Understand the situation;

make different choices for yourself.

When you practice this, you will begin to develop an automatic inner control of difficult situations. You raise your awareness of yourself and of your interactions with others. Work diligently with this for a couple of weeks and you will see how your perceptions and reactions begin to change.

[For a more in-depth perspective and slightly different approach on how to use this process for self-growth see Appendix II.]

Questions and Ideas for Contemplation

The best measure of your self-worth is how you feel. When negativity of any kind affects you – worry, anger, blame, guilt, frustration, etc. – your ego is at play and your self-worth, unless you rise to the occasion, may take a hit. That is why self-awareness plays such an important role – because it allows us the opportunity to maintain control while we deal with the many concerns that come into our purview as managers and leaders without losing our belief in and understanding of self. The self we wish to be as a manager, leader, and as a human being.

Pay close attention to your feelings during any difficulties you encounter.

> How do you feel afterward?

> How do you feel you handled the situation?

> How well were you able to maintain control in the face of problems you had to deal with?

If you do this for several weeks, you will understand yourself better because you will have learned how different concerns affect you at work And you will have gained better control of your ability to respond intelligently and kindly while maintaining your own self-value.

A great personal building exercise

Go back to the first part of this chapter and answer each of the questions listed under the subtitle "How do you feel about yourself." Do this in writing and try to be completely open and honest about each answer. Write until you say everything you need to say. Come back to these a week or so later and see if you have anything to add to any of your answers. Then take some time over the next few weeks and consider your answers carefully. You will have established a good foundation for what you feel good about and what you may need a bit more insight and self-work on.

Revisit this in a year and see if you have made any changes in how you approach your work life and how you feel about yourself in relation to work and others.

Chapter 12

Self-Confidence

Confidence – 1. Firm belief; trust; reliance 2. The fact of being or feeling certain; assurance 3. Belief in one's own abilities; self-confidence (*Webster's New World Dictionary*)

Self-confidence – confidence in oneself, one's own abilities (*Webster's New World Dictionary*)

Self-confidence is rooted in your self-value – your Self-Worth. It is partially the outward manifestation of how you feel about yourself at any given moment as you interact with others and deal with all the trials and tribulations you encounter at work. It is also the self-assuredness you feel in dealing with problems and concerns.

Assertiveness

Self-confident people approach others from an assertive stance. Assertiveness is being able to maintain control of oneself in an interaction with another person – regardless of their behavior. This is especially critical when dealing with difficult behaviors and difficult circumstances.

> Demanding, bossy, directive, controlling, pushy, 'I'm always right' behaviors are **aggressive** in nature. While they may be effective in getting things done, they reflect insecurity and fear on the part of the manager who uses them to rule the roost. They also tend to create a negative, non-creative, ego-driven aura in the workplace.

> Defensive, behind-the-back, surreptitious, and laissez-faire behaviors also reflect insecurity and fear, but use non-directive means of getting people to do things – these are **passive-aggressive** and **passive** behaviors. Managers who use such tactics often hold things over people's heads

as a means of getting things done. These types of behaviors create an atmosphere of underlying tension and subterfuge that undermines everyone's self-worth.

An assertive leader has a handle on his/her own emotions and how they may impact others, and, importantly, understands that other people's emotional investment in an issue that may affect how they come across. Quality leadership means using your emotions and intellect to <u>guide</u> the choices you make rather than letting those emotions <u>control</u> how you act.

[The process delineated at the end of the previous chapter (See "The Self-Awareness – Self-worth process") and in more detail in Appendix II, "Being in Control," helps us develop our self-awareness, our self-worth, and our self-confidence in difficult situations. When we practice this, we can choose to respond assertively to others' negativity, rather than aggressively or passively.]

Believe in your own abilities

Your abilities got you into the role you have today. Use those strengths to establish a confidence in your own work and in your team's approach. Be willing to admit where you have limitations. Use the strengths of others, as well as a willingness to learn and grow, to further create an atmosphere where trust and reliance of each other rules, rather than playing 'one-upmanship' or 'I'm better than you' games and intrigue.

When you can own up to foibles and inadequacies, it does not make you 'less than' or weaker; it makes you stronger. In many ways a willingness to admit to being less than perfect and having areas you are working on helps to enhance your many strengths. You also become more of a real person to your employees. When you can be open about who you are and what you bring to the table, you will develop trust and respect.

People respect the truth.

Respect

Respect is not something garnered by trying to be or act perfect. We respect people who are open, honest, and down-to-earth. There is a certain assurance we feel in being with someone who doesn't hide behind a façade. We like to know 'where they are coming from.' (See also Chapter 13, "Honesty")

We respect them for respecting who we are and what is important to us. We like people to accept us for our own efforts and for our ideas. It is important to us that our boss makes an effort to understand what is important to us and why. She doesn't necessarily have to agree with us; but we sincerely appreciate her effort to listen and understand.

We respect them for how they treat us, especially if we feel they are considerate of us as human beings first, and employees second. Acknowledgement is a key skill and tool for working with all people. It is an especially useful tool to use in difficult circumstances with someone. Throw in a good dose of appreciation and you probably will not have very many difficult people concerns in your camp.

Employees like to feel that they have a leader they can have confidence in. Who you are, what you believe in, what you do, what you say, and how you treat others, sets the stage for how you are perceived. Even in those circumstances where you may not feel as confident as you would like, creating an aura of confidence through your actions and words sets the tone for everyone else. This can be especially important during times of change or other difficulties.

Leadership is fundamentally about leading. How you lead – the overall confidence you show to others and help instill in others can make all the difference in weathering workplace crises. You create that on a day-to-day basis by how you interact with people. You instill it in others when you maintain that confidence in spite of whatever troubles may arise.

Confidence is about showing the way.

What are you showing to your employees?

Questions and Ideas for Contemplation

How would you answer the following questions? Take some time to consider them in some depth as they will help you develop a broader understanding of yourself as a manager and leader.

> How confident are you in handling the many different relationships, interactions, and managerial tasks you have at work?

> If you pay close attention to your feelings of self-worth and self-confidence for a week, what do you notice about the ebb and flow of your emotions?

> What types of circumstances or behaviors seem to affect you more than others?

> What techniques do you use to maintain control (self-control) during periods of frustration or stress?

> How do these tactics impact others?

> Can you make wiser choices?

Know yourself – the key to being the best leader you can be.

Chapter 13

Self-Control

To be great is not to be placed above humanity, ruling others,

but to stand above the partialities and futilities of uninformed

desire, and to rule one's self.

(Spinoza/Durant)

[Author's Note: I used this same quote to open a similar discussion in my book, *Succeeding with Difficult Bosses*. This perspective is important from all viewpoints!]

Controlling others is an illusion

Some bosses attempt to control others by being demanding, aggressive, dictatorial, etc. They may seem to be in control, but given an out or some breathing room and their employees will fly the coop. If you use any type of negative, force-driven (command and control) form of management you might achieve some success as a directive manager, but you won't be a leader – **leadership implies a willingness for others to follow**.

The only true control is self-control

Developing the ability to maintain control of your emotions and reactions in even difficult situations sets a powerful example for others. Great leaders ARE emotional and even passionate about what they do and what they believe in. They have learned to handle their emotions with intelligent design. They control their emotions by choosing to respond to concerns rather than reacting with little or no restraint to negativity.

> Author's Note: I remember very vividly a scene from a high school basketball game – a scene that impressed upon me the incredible power of **self** control.

The stage was set when a player on our home team was driving to the basket for a lay-up. Then the referee blew his whistle and called a foul on him. It was a poor call, as the other player had clearly stepped in front of this home-town favorite and blocked his lane at the last second. The player, ball palmed in his hand, rushed up to the referee. Raising the ball high over his head, he brought it swiftly around and down as if to slam the ball onto the floor. Instead he stopped the powerful motion and placed the ball carefully and gently on the wooden floor at the referee's feet and gave it a pat, turning away toward his bench as he did so.

This showed remarkable restraint in an otherwise volatile atmosphere where this particular referee's calls had seemed to all go one way during the game. This one small element of personal control helped to ease the crowd's tension as everyone laughed, and yet, the gesture, non-violent and controlled, told the referee exactly how the young man felt without him losing control, and likely, being tossed from the game.

Difficult People

When one person can remain calm and in-control in a difficult situation with others, it creates an entirely different atmosphere, and typically, a different chain of events than if everyone is simply reacting. This is particularly true when one of the individuals maintaining control is an authority figure.

It sets an example

It maintains a sense of stability and control

It creates a focal point that others can gather to

It gives others a foundation upon which to garner and maintain their own self worth, self-confidence, and self-control

Keep in mind that all people, especially those with a low self-worth, have a tremendous need to feel in control. You can often give people a sense of power and control by helping them feel involved and by giving them venues where they feel they can contribute ideas, make suggestions, air concerns, etc. (See Chapter 6, "Walk, Listen, Learn, Follow-Up")

Do you have a troublemaker in your group?

Help them to feel needed, involved, and to have a sense of control of their workspace. You might be very surprised at how quickly they may begin to move out of their negative approach to work and begin adding more to your team. Above all else, learn to listen to them respectfully. Show them that they and their ideas are valued.

Power and Control

As a manager you have power. You may have the power to make or break an employee. You probably have the power to make many decisions, to hire, to fire, to give evaluations, to handle a budget, etc. If you are wise, you will use your power to involve individuals, to empower them, and to create a workspace that lets them know you will use your personal power and the trust given to you to the best of your ability for them and for the team.

If you use power wisely, you will very likely have few control issues.

Empowering others

Involving others, giving them a sense of ownership of key issues and decisions, helps them to feel a part of the power structure of a team. They will know that the buck stops at your door and that you will still have to make final and sometimes hard decisions. Keep in mind though, that the perception of power and how it is used (and one's ability to feel a part of the decisions made with that power) creates a vastly different aura within a team than one formed by a manager who handles everything himself, ignores other people's concerns and advice, directs and demands, and micro-manages.

Listening is one of the most basic and yet empowering skills you can develop.

Communicating without making judgments is another.

If you are willing to give responsibility to others and to empower them to make decisions, you will encourage a creative, dynamic, learning work environment which will become a powerful tool in your arsenal for being the best leader you can be.

Questions and Ideas for Contemplation

Some managers hoard power and are afraid that to give anyone any responsibility or jurisdiction will take away from their ability to control their team and workspace. The opposite is actually the truth. Your people, given the space, trust, and responsibility they deserve, will help empower you.

> How can you empower your people?

> What specific actions can you take today that help your team members feel more in-control of their work lives and work space?

Often there are a great many things we can offer others without giving up any power or control, and in the process we gain powerful personal and team-building commitments from our personnel.

Chapter 14

Honesty

"Truth is the most valuable thing we have. Let us economize it."

(Mark Twain)

The Truth is – it is hard to be completely open and honest

in today's business climate.

We have to try harder!

(Koob)

Telling the truth is also only part of the battle. The true test of leadership is how you treat people, and that entails being willing (and able) to be open about everything feasible in the work place, especially the 'bad' stuff.

"To thine own self be true..." (*Hamlet*, William Shakespeare)

Honesty starts with and is about who we are and the 'who' we bring to work with us. Honesty starts with self-awareness and is founded in our key values and qualities. When we are able to stay within ourselves and maintain our self-control we bring TRUTH to work with us. (See Chapter 4, "Integrity, Ownership, Responsibility"; Chapter 9, "Self-Awareness; and Chapter 10, "Self-Worth")

If managers and leaders take a close look at their work environment, culture, and interactions, it is not hard to find subtle and not-so-subtle examples of subterfuge, hidden agendas, close-to-the-chest mentality, behind-the-back dealings, etc. at work. Avoiding these types of pitfalls and bringing everything more out in the open are keys to successful management. Many of the difficulties perpetrated by disgruntled, 'difficult' employees fester behind the scenes. Part of your job as a leader is to negate these difficulties by creating an atmosphere where they cannot easily exist.

If we are really willing to look at how we interact with others, we will very likely find that we could be even more open in our work with them without compromising anything or anyone. It does take courage, and it takes a commitment to being as honest and open as is feasible. You have to be willing to make changes in this arena. However, when we ARE willing to make this commitment and effort, these types of subterfuge will have no place to take root. Keep in mind that people often mimic what they see and experience. When you are open and honest and you insist on others following suit, there is little room for, or interest in, clandestine office behavior.

> "The Principle difference between a cat and a lie
>
> is that a cat only has nine lives."
>
> (Mark Twain)

Beyond telling the truth

When we make an effort to be fully honest with ourselves, we also make a commitment to others. The two go hand in hand. However, simply being willing to tell the truth is only part of the effort we must put forth.

Honesty is also about

Keeping people informed – employees will often feel that when they are not kept in the loop, that they are being mistreated, or even 'lied to.' Other feelings employees may have if their manager uses poor or close-to-the-chest communications:

> Poor self-image; feeling less than; put down; or second rate

> Unmotivated

> Unacknowledged and unappreciated

> Not important

> Frustration and anger which becomes tension and stress

Honesty is also about

Being willing to communicate the bad news as well as good news – if you can't or won't communicate bad news or be willing to talk about difficult topics with your people, they will question your integrity. You will face a loss of trust. Not knowing something can be far more damaging to someone and to a work environment than the bad news itself.

Communicating what can't be shared – managers make the mistake of keeping silent when things are going on that will affect their employees but can't be shared yet because of corporate caveats. It is a key leadership skill to let people know what you can and **can't** share:

> "I want everyone to know that I will give you the best information I have on the changes being considered by this administration as soon as I am given the go-ahead. As you know I have certain restrictions placed on what I can share with you. I promise I will keep you as up-to-date as I am able and as soon as I have a green light I will fill in any gaps. In the meantime let us all be proactive about maintaining our commitment and focus. I will make an effort to answer as many of your questions as I can, but please keep in mind that there are some topics that are currently taboo because things haven't been finalized. I appreciate your understanding and patience through this difficult time."

During difficult change processes a good leader may have to reiterate this type of message to his/her troops on a regular basis. People want to know you are on top of things and that you WILL keep them informed. Reassurances are always welcome and will help keep the rumor mills running at slower speeds.

Honesty is also about

Avoiding secrets, hidden agendas, and other subtle behaviors that shut people out – just about everything in an office eventually becomes public knowledge one way or another. Maintaining an open, sharing atmosphere minimizes the back-door politics that are often a part of situations created by unhappy people. People who feel they are treated fairly and who understand the dynamics of a situation, no matter how difficult, will be more willing to weather changes and they are more likely to stay motivated and working as productive team members throughout.

Honesty and Kindness

Honesty should always be tempered with kindness. Tact is a necessary skill to possess if you are in a leadership position. But people can easily see through a 'skill' to the heart of the matter. Tact coupled with kindness is an ideal approach to dealing with difficult situations, but keep in mind that kindness is the key ingredient.

By observing our thoughts and communications with others we can choose far better ways to express things.

> Author's Note: As an executive coach and mentor I am often asked how to say things that have to be said in 'better,' 'kinder,' and more positive ways. I typically work with my clients by helping them to discover the best ways to say things that are difficult or awkward to communicate. With this give-and-take process these leaders learn to develop the important skill of combining kindness with whatever they need to impart to their team members and it becomes much easier for them to maintain their openness and honesty. It pays major dividends throughout their careers.

Both our verbal and written communications can be improved with a little kindness. Here is a short example that shows how a few changes can make all the difference in the world. I actually received this note from the admissions office at a university when I was a graduate assistant:

> "Take John Doe from your roll. He is dead."

This would have been better:

> "Please take John Doe off of your roll. He passed away recently."

And better:

> "I need to inform you that one of your students, John Doe, passed away. Please make sure to take him off of your roll."

And better yet,

> "I regretfully need to inform you that one of your students,

John Doe, passed away recently. Please make sure you do not include him in your final class roll. Thanks."

Needless to say as a new graduate student I was shocked to read the first version above when I received it. I would still have been sad if I had received the latter version, but it would have hit me considerably less hard!

The important idea here is that our language does provide for kinder, more compassionate ways to say things. The wise leader makes sure they are part of his/her repertoire when concerns are addressed.

You can begin to develop your skills by **paying attention to how you communicate**, especially in difficult situations, and, very importantly, **by observing how what you say impacts others**, i.e. how do they react?

Brevity ad Kindness

Being kind does not take much time or space – it is more often about HOW you approach things. I can add a simple acknowledgement, a thank you, even a compliment to a 'to-the-point' e-mail or memo that only a takes a few seconds more and very little space.

In verbal communications rephrasing a blunt statement and adding a supportive sentiment takes almost no additional time. The only caveat is that you learn how to add these kindnesses to your daily repertoire.

A Key Skill

One of the easiest and best ways to keep things above board when things are going on behind the scenes is to **ask**.

> "John, I heard there are some concerns about how the Johnston contract is coming together. I would like to sit down with you, Beth, and Ron to discuss all the ramifications to date. I have set a meeting for three today. Bring your list of concerns and we'll hammer this out. Thanks. Keep up the good work on the data you're collecting."

If John has been griping, blaming, and spreading general negativity, you have just opened the door to dealing with his concerns. Even if he tends to be a regular whiner, when you use this approach several times, he will get the message fairly quickly that you won't put up with behind-the-scenes negativity. This statement opens doors for discussion, gets key players together, and has no blame or negativity attached. You even take the opportunity to throw in a 'Thank you,' and a compliment.

Asking gives people an open venue in which to air concerns. It can stop rumor-mongering and complaining quickly if handled judiciously. It is also a way of acknowledging and appreciating people's need to be understood.

> "Brenda, I understand you are upset with something that happened in the meeting yesterday. Tell me what's on your mind and we'll work through this. I want you to feel like you can come to me when you have these types of concerns. I am here for you and the whole team, so let's work this out."

Stay in touch – "Walk, Listen, Learn, Follow-up" (see Chapter 6) and you will have far fewer difficult situations to deal with. Be willing to ask when concerns arise and you will nip many other potential difficulties in the bud.

Don't have the time for this kind of stuff?

You can't afford not to find the time because you will be dealing with far more serious concerns down the road if you don't deal with concerns openly and honestly.

The Keys to Honest Leadership

> Be your truth – the 'who' you bring to the table sets the stage for your team
>
> Tell the truth – whenever you can
>
> Tell them when you can't be open about matters of concern – keep them in the loop
>
> Insist on an open honest atmosphere -- through your example and helping everyone keep things above-board
>
> Ask – Asking shows a willingness to listen and understand, and helps you set a team atmosphere that helps to keep things above board. It also shows a person respect.

Questions and Ideas for Contemplation

Learning to observe our own communication patterns and to subsequently make an effort to be more open, honest, and kind, is hard work. It takes practice and a long term commitment. Your success will show in individual and team spirit and in your interactions on the job.

It is particularly useful to observe how you react and communicate in difficult circumstances. These will show your true mettle as a leader.

Set a goal each week to consciously observe the subtleties of your communications with others. You may be surprised at how much you notice that you may not have been aware of and how easy it is to make little changes in how you approach others – and in particular in difficult communication concerns.

To finish Shakespeare's quote:

"To Thine own Self be True,

and it shall follow, as the night, the day,

That Thou canst not then be False to any Man."

(Hamlet)

Chapter 15

Kindness and Compassion

Kindness Takes Courage

Unfortunately some managers equate being kind and compassionate with weakness. They seem to be afraid that if they show anything but a firm, in-control exterior that employees will take advantage of every opportunity to usurp power. The truth is that true power is in self-control and in an assertive approach to difficulties. Maintaining power through the rigid control of others is not leadership, nor is it very smart.

Kindness can work wonders, and it may be one of the best skills you can develop to avoid difficulties arising and to help keep your team on track. People appreciate even small gestures. Sometimes these are the key to turning someone's day or week around.

"What care I how simple it be, if it be not ever so simple to me."

(Ben Jonson)

I can think of dozens of 'small' and 'simple' gestures that people have done for me that literally made all the difference in my day. Here is one example. A recent, true story:

> My wife was informed that the company she was working for was shutting down the entire plant where we lived. Three thousand people would be out of work, not to mention the waves of peripheral economic impact that would hit this moderately-sized community.

> The day after this hard news hit us I went to a new and popular ice cream store to drown my upset (because it meant we would be moving again) in a big goopy ice cream sundae. While the young man was making my sundae, we chatted and I mentioned that my wife had been

affected by the big shutdown. He commiserated somewhat awkwardly, as one would expect a teenager to do.

I guess, figuring we would be in financial difficulty as a result of this closure and my wife's subsequent job loss, this high school student told me he was going to give me his twenty-percent store discount....That stopped me in my tracks! I was floored. What a wonderful gesture – totally out of the blue. (It was probably all of eighty cents!)

I went home thinking about how easy it is for someone to help make someone else feel better. I decided to give him a copy of one of my books with five new twenty dollar bills enclosed toward college. Unfortunately, even though I made a special effort to go by that store many times, I never saw him again.

It IS the simple things that matter – and that young man helped remind me that I can make a difference every day.

Do a simple, kind thing for someone – your heart will be glad you did. Do them on a regular basis with/for your team members (and everyone up and down the chain and across matrices) and you will have a much more enjoyable work life with far fewer people concerns.

The simple things matter

Thanking people honors them and you

A kind word can make a day brighter

A compliment may bring a big smile

Asking someone what they care about shows compassion

Listening and making an effort to understand acknowledges another person

Adding a personal touch to your communications may be the kindest thing you can do for someone who is struggling with personal concerns

Personal recognition for small wins is often far more inspiring than celebrations for major successes

Pay attention to your people and you will learn what and how to make a positive difference in their work lives. You will know what is right when you get a smile and a sincere thank you in response.

"Compassion is kindness in the most difficult of circumstances."

(Koob)

Problems do happen

There are always (ALWAYS!) kinder ways to deal with difficulties:

> Being firm is sometimes necessary – couple it with kindness and compassion and you are a person, not just a manager

> Being 'the boss' is also sometimes important – you can still lead, show strength and courage, make hard decisions and still be caring and kind

> Resolving conflict is a common part of management and leadership – do it kindly and compassionately and people will remember you as a leader, not just as a manager of difficulties.

> Don't forget to ask – kindly and compassionately. It shows acknowledgement and appreciation for the people you work with.

> Being right is nice, but it is not always necessary. Examine your motivations and consider kindness in the decisions you make as well as in who needs to be right. Being right almost always has to do with ego and very little to do with our self-worth. Giving up the need to be right means you are rooted in your self-worth and are open to listening to others.

Wisdom is the birthright of those who are kind;

not of those who need to be right all the time.

Remember that you don't have to agree with someone, but offering them the kindness of listening carefully to what they have to say will help them to feel right in another sense.

We have all had a few of those!

We have all been through tough times in life. Maybe the difficult person you are working with is dealing with personal burdens that you have only seen a glimpse of. You can make a difference – sometimes a huge difference. The beauty of kindness is that when you make a difference with one person, it will infect your whole team and then there is that ripple effect which will infect others as well.

A kind gesture may be the one thing that can help turn a person's day around.

Kindness may be the catalyst for helping turn someone's week round.

Heartfelt Understanding, Kindness, and Compassion may be all that is needed to help begin to turn someone's life around.

Wow!

One of the great things about kindness is

that it doesn't have to cost anything

and it pays huge dividends!

Talk about cost effectiveness!

Questions and Ideas for Contemplation

People respond to how they are treated. Sometimes it is tough to find the positive when there are so many difficulties to deal with. Change and upheaval do tend to bring out the worst in people. You can make a difference by working the other end of the spectrum. Commit to small random acts of kindness on a regular basis.

When things get tough, double or triple those efforts.

Start today and commit to spreading some kindness throughout your team. Keep your finger on the overall aura on your team for the next few weeks as you do this. See what a difference it can make, and then take stock of how you are feeling. You might be surprised to find you are less stressed and more in control than ever!

(See also Chapter 17, "Taking Care of Your People.")

Chapter 16

Positivity

Negativity breeds Negativity

Positivity breeds Positivity

Choose Wisely

If you, as a leader, have your hand on the pulse of your team, you know what the prevalent atmosphere is. If it isn't where you want it to be, you have work to do. Even when you are thrust into a situation that is less than ideal there are many things you can do to turn negativity around.

Positivity trumps negativity every time

You don't have to be a bubbling, outgoing, always 'up' personality. You can still make a difference. It does take commitment to being positive in the face of negativity. It takes persistence. And it takes maintaining your own self-worth in spite of the difficulties you are facing.

A true story

I once took over a department that had a notoriously bad reputation throughout the entire organization. Things were so bad that when I called another department and asked for something, I typically got the cold shoulder or at best a half-hearted willingness to help. It was as if people expected me (my department) to be demanding, pushy, unappreciative, unfriendly, and negative. No one was enthusiastic about my being there except my boss and the few higher ups who had been involved in my hiring. No one wanted anything to do with my department.

Whatever had transpired prior to my taking that job had set a very negative stage. I knew some of this going into the job, but it was still a bit of a shock to experience it first hand.

A year and a half later every department in that organization would bend over backwards to help us out.

What changed?

Was I able to wave a magic wand and everything suddenly got better?

Not really. It was hard work on my part with the support of my boss and my boss' boss.

Basically I started out by treating people in other departments how I wanted my department and team to be treated.

I had to weather a lot of negativity. Much of the time it was bearing up under the weight of it and re-grouping on my own time. While I made some initial mistakes, I knew I needed to avoid defensive reactions and any negativity in working with other team leaders and teams even when what I was facing was disgruntledness, defensiveness, and verbal attacks.

I had to watch what I said and how I said it. In the first months, even neutral statements I made were sometimes taken by other department heads as negative. I learned to adjust what I needed to convey so that I said it is as positive a way as possible. I also had to watch carefully for how things I said and did were taken. Perceptions on the part of the people I engaged were everything for this learning curve.

I listened, got to know what motivated other department heads, and asked a lot of questions. I especially tried to focus on what I could do for them even when I was seeking help from their area.

Most importantly, I added positivity whenever and with whomever I could:

> I said 'Thank you' often – on the phone, in person, through e-mails, in memos. I made sure they knew I appreciated everything they did for my team.

> I followed up initial 'thanks' with a written note and made it a point to call up a department head to thank them if someone on their team assisted my team. This took some time, but over the long haul I saved myself and my team a good bit of frustration and difficulty. And ultimately it

helped me get things done quickly and efficiently when the other team heads began to trust me and what I was trying to accomplish.

I gave compliments at every opportunity. If the opportunities didn't obviously present themselves, I found ways to get positivity and a pat on the back into the mix.

For example:

> If the maintenance crew came over to fix something in my building (one of the many teams that was at odds with my department), I made it a point to personally thank the men that did the work; called their boss and thanked them for a great job; and followed up with a written thank you memo through the system. If I felt it was appropriate, I would send a copy of appreciation for work well done to that team leader's boss.

I stayed on top of what they wanted from me and I would go out of my way to touch base with one department or another on a regular basis to see if they needed any information from me or my team. I also made sure I got things my team was asked to accomplish done expeditiously. Whenever feasible I made sure we double and triple checked the quality of everything we provided other teams.

It did take awhile. There was a good bit of ingrained lack of trust with my area and while some people responded fairly quickly to my efforts, other areas seemed reluctant to believe that I was truly a different manager than the person I had replaced.

I also made mistakes along the way and had to learn as I was going. Simply understanding the difficulties I was facing with certain departments and individuals was time consuming. The hardest part was keeping a firm grip on my own self-worth in the midst of the general negativity I encountered. I had to fully commit to a positive course of action and stick to it regardless of what came my way.

When we (I) made a mistake, I learned to apologize and then make every effort to make up for it. Part of the success we enjoined was due to immediately being willing to jump on top of anything that wasn't right and fix it.

When in doubt, I asked. I asked for:

> What they needed
>
> What I could do for them
>
> To understand
>
> For clarification
>
> For anything and everything that would help get and keep the lines of communication open

While I am far from an effusive glad-hander, committing to positivity made the difference. It was a day-to-day, week-to-week, month-to-month effort until it became natural for me and until they came to expect it.

What happened long term?

I got a lot of thanks and support from the people on my team and from people across the organization. Though this leadership role is now some time behind me, if I hear from someone from those bygone days, they often mention the positive influence I had. While it was a lot of hard work, I am glad to have been able to leave that kind of legacy.

What are you bringing to work?

Careful self-observation can tell you what you need to know about how people perceive you. Think carefully about the following – all of these will be perceived by others as negative:

> Blaming
>
> Complaining
>
> Being down; depressed – any negative affect
>
> Anxiety, stress
>
> Worry – when we worry, people notice. Worry increases our stress levels and it negatively impacts others whether we realize it or not.
>
> Anger, upset, perturbation
>
> Moodiness

When you exhibit these behaviors at work, people will notice. As a leader, you will **infect** your troops; particularly if you carry any negativity around with you for any extended period of time. (Yes, even a few hours!).

The next two chapters of this book are aimed directly at positive things you can do at work for yourself, your coworkers, and for your team members that make a difference.

Infusing positivity into your work life is all about survival on one level – keeping on top of negativity and difficulties – and about you and your team members enjoying their work life on the other. A great many difficulties in the work place could be avoided if we consciously commit to adding our positive slant to what we do at every opportunity. You CAN make a difference. When you do, people will see you as a leader, not just a manager.

Questions and Ideas for Contemplation

Start by knowing the people you are working with – understanding who they are and what they want, need, and desire; what they bring to the table; and what they expect of you. Then dive in with both feet and find ways to add positivity to the mix. When you have done your homework, you will know how and with whom you need to place your efforts.

If in doubt, be willing to ask. It is a form of acknowledgement of the importance of someone else's ideas and perspective and it shows an appreciation of who they are as a person and colleague.

In general, the key is finding ways to put positive effort into everything you do. Positivity does trump negativity, but you have to stick to your guns!

Chapter 17

Taking Care of Your People

"I need to get down to the office and take care of my people."

In Memoriam – Dad

(Colonel Robert A. Koob, US Army, Ret.)

You have probably heard the statement, "When you take care of your people, they will take care of you." While sometimes it may not feel this way in this helter-skelter, 'everyone for themself' world, this is as close to the truth as you can get. Leaders need to Care.

Much of this book to this point has been about the many things that go into developing a leadership style that focuses on people. The reasons are manifold, but when you get down to brass tacks it is all about making the most of the situation you are in. The best way I know how to do that is to be proactive with people rather than reactive to problems that occur.

By being proactive you mitigate troubles before they can get off the ground. When you take care of your people, when you care for them, you will have far fewer personnel issues, period.

Yes, sometimes you will have to deal with conflicts and difficulties. That is the focus of the second half of this book. However, isn't it worth spending some extra time with your team to ensure that these types of concerns are minimal?

Even when you find yourself entering a situation where difficulties already exist, you can make a difference almost immediately by focusing on people – who they are, what is important to them, what they want, what they need, and what they care about.

Who are they?

Walk, Listen, Learn, Follow-up (WLLF) is first and foremost about getting to know your people not only as workers on a team striving toward specific goals, but as people. When you make this kind of effort people feel acknowledged. [See Chapter 6]

This does take some time, but the time you spend learning something about the people you work with is time you probably won't have to spend fixing problems and concerns.

This is one of those ideas that most people love...to think about...but when push comes to shove they just can't afford the time. The truth is, **you cannot afford not to find the time**. If you find yourself saying, "I will, I will. Maybe tomorrow," and tomorrow just never seems to get there, then you need to do some serious soul searching about whether you want to be just a good manager or a great leader.

And it doesn't stop there – no matter what level you are on or how busy your schedule is, this should be at the very least a weekly affair – not just a 'Once a year I will try to get out there' sort of thing. And here is a big caveat – town hall meetings, luncheons with the troops, one-on-ones don't count. Don't get me wrong, these can be valuable too, but they're not WLLF or MBWA. [If you want the whole scoop, read almost any of Tom Peters works, especially *A Passion for Excellence* (Peters and Austin) Management By Wandering Around.]

What is important to them?

One of the most important techniques you can develop as a leader is to ask. Asking acknowledges a person. When you sincerely listen, it shows appreciation for who they are and what is important to them. Part of this skill is in learning to ask, and then listen without judgments of any kind entering the mix (also a key to using Walk, Listen, Learn, and Follow-up – successfully).

Learn to ask open-ended questions, and then listen carefully to how someone responds. Avoid directing the conversation by jumping in to answer, offer advice (unless answering a specific request), qualifying what they say, etc. First and foremost, just listen. You will gain tremendous insight into your players and they will learn to see you as a person, not just as a manager, evaluator, director, demander, etc.

"Glad to see you've gotten moved into your new office space Tom. Anything you need from me?"

"Betty, how is the new job going? Anything I can do for you?"

"Hi Gene, thought I'd stop by and see how you were doing? Any problems or concerns?"

"Bob, glad I caught you. How are the kids? Wife?"

There are a myriad of ways to open things up. Find your comfort zone and then try different approaches. What works with one person, may not get much of a response from another. Some people you might have to spend some time drawing out, as they will shy away from opening up to an authority figure initially. Be patient and try again if all you get is "Nope, I'm good." It may take a few weeks or longer for people to understand that you really do want to know what is on their minds and that you will make a difference whenever feasible with their concerns.

It can be difficult at first to learn not to make judgments or offer long-winded explanations or rebuttals. Focus on letting them say what is important to them. When appropriate, answer queries as briefly as possible. Anything that needs more attention should probably be deferred until later. You want the focus to remain on them and their issues. Don't forget to thank them for whatever they offer.

If an issue is raised that needs considerably more focus, set up a more formal meeting. Be sure to follow-up on any important issues they raise. You don't always have to agree or even succeed at filling requests. The important thing is that they have had a chance to be heard and that you are willing to make an effort, where feasible, to support them and what they want.

What do they want?

Employees are often shy and/or hesitant about asking for what they want. You may not be able to provide everything their heart desires, but you can listen. Listening sincerely to what people believe they want and need acknowledges them. Be honest about what is or is not possible. When people have a chance to be heard, the getting of their 'wants' may not be so important after all.

"Carol, I hear what you are saying and you are right. We need that equipment to kick up our production. However, I'm not sure that will be feasible considering the budget constraints this quarter. Let's keep it on the table. Why don't you do a cost analysis and we'll discuss it at the next team meeting."

"Ted, I have to be honest with you. I don't think upper management will buy this kind of approach, though I really like your creative thinking on this problem. Keep it up. I like to hear new ideas and we will definitely consider anything you come up with that seems good for the team and organization. Good job."

"I looked into your request to change vendors for the 'x' widget, Steve. It was a good call on the pricing. Unfortunately, I found out that they require a minimum purchase of ten thousand units a month and a long-term commitment of two years to get that price. As you know, we use less than half that amount. Keep digging though – that is how we find ways to save money around here. Thanks for the heads up on this one. It was worth a shot."

What do they need?

What people want may not always equate with what they need. Careful (and sometimes creative) listening and probing can help you understand what really needs to be focused on. Solutions to even age-old problems can come from the least likely sources. Use this type of quality time with your employees to understand what they need to step up their job productivity and enjoyment, as well as the quality of the goods or services you provide.

The keys to Taking Care of Your People

Acknowledge

Appreciate

Recognize

Reward

Acknowledgement

The most powerful personnel tool you have is your ability to let your people know you care. You do that by spending some quality time with them in their space – not just in your office, a town hall meeting, or a group luncheon. These types of get-togethers all have purpose, but they don't acknowledge an individual. Your direct personal communications – in-person, e-mail, phone, memos, announcements, etc. – are great ways to acknowledge them and their ideas.

Acknowledging your team players only costs you a bit of your time. Time that is well spent when you consider the concerns you will probably take care of, and those that will never develop all because you made an effort to get to know your people.

Appreciation

We all like to be appreciated for who we are and what we do. The most powerful forms of appreciation are often the simplest and least expensive. Appreciate people at every opportunity – make it a habit!

> Learn to 'thank' people often – it is the best way to appreciate someone
>
> Sincere words of appreciation for small wins are powerful:
>
> > "Great job on that poster, Ruth. I loved it!"
>
> Words of encouragement work equally well:
>
> > "Keep up the good work, Ron."
>
> Small gestures or tokens of appreciation can be especially powerful– a flower, a lunch, movie tickets, in-team award – whatever you and they will be comfortable with

Recognition

Acknowledgement and Appreciation are often aimed at an individual. Recognition implies that we are acknowledging and appreciating someone or a group more globally, in front of others. Often the simplest forms of recognition are the most powerful:

> "Jean, I wanted to acknowledge your contribution to this effort in front of the team, because you were the key person in bringing home this contract for us. Kudos!"

"What a great job everyone did on the product 'X' development. Special thanks to 'A' and 'B' teams for bringing this to fruition. A great group effort! We are adding this plaque recognizing this division's efforts to the factory wall of fame. Come on up here Betty and Bob and please accept management's heartfelt thanks for a job well done."

Verbal recognition in front of peers and to higher-ups means a great deal to an individual or team.

E-mail, memos, certificates, and formal letters of commendation are also great ways to let people know you appreciate who they are and what they have accomplished.

Reward

We tend to think of rewards in business today in financial terms, but people feel rewarded when you make an effort to acknowledge, appreciate, and recognize them. You can take this a step further and have more formal rewards and ceremonies. These can also be very positive motivators.

The danger with formal awards – bonuses are good examples – is that they can be as much de-motivators as motivators. Be judicious in setting parameters for rewards and make an effort to be sure everyone has an opportunity to win over the long haul.

Formal awards should probably be team or organization-managed and have very specific parameters.

However, it is possible to have small in-team awards that everyone recognizes and accepts as part of a job well done. Examples might include:

A luncheon for the successful completion of a project

Small recognitions – plaques, certificates, etc. – for jobs completed/done well

Gift certificates

Use your imagination.

[Note: See Appendix I for a discussion of "Handling Employee Evaluations."]

Important

The best forms of acknowledgement, appreciation, recognition, and reward come spontaneously from you. It shows you are paying attention, that they matter, and that you care.

Questions and Ideas for Contemplation

When you know your team members, you build a foundation for success. From that knowledge you have the opportunity to "take care of your people" by showing appreciation throughout the year.

Take some time to consider what you feel will work the best with your team members. You may want to focus for a week or two on consciously making an effort to acknowledge and appreciate people in different ways. Then try to jump off from that and make it a habit.

Chapter 18

Taking Care of Yourself

To tell you the truth I have seen far too many overworked, over-stressed, and very-close-to-burnt-out managers in today's business environs. While I know that in some ways it is the name of the game today; you do have choices you can make that can make things better. The bottom line is what you bring to work and what you bring to your interactions with everyone at work – your SELF. If you are stressed, down, and burnt-out, it will rub off on your team players and everyone else you work with. It is worth really thinking about.

What you can do?

Learn to accept responsibility for the YOU you bring to work.

Make a commitment to managing your time – your work-life balance. There are many people who do care and many who you do affect when you are constantly working with very little down-time, quality time, relationship time, and family time.

Take care of yourself when you are stressed, down, etc.

Be willing to get support and help when needed (we all need it sometimes!)

You

The first part of this book is about how you can make a difference from the get-go. A major emphasis is on **Self Awareness**. By staying on top of how you feel, what you are thinking, and how you come across to others, you give yourself the opportunity AND permission to acknowledge yourself when you do feel out of sorts.

But it doesn't stop with recognition. You also have to be willing to step back and make changes. The most important part of this is to be willing to say to yourself, "Okay, I'm getting a bit over the edge here. I need to..." And what follows should be a personal commitment to take better care of yourself. And that should be followed by some real specifics that you WILL make a sincere effort to inculcate into your life.

By acknowledging your status quo and by making a commitment to do something, you automatically change the dynamics of how you will impact others at work. It doesn't necessarily take a major time commitment to make changes either, but it DOES take doing what is necessary **as soon as possible** before you impact someone else negatively. It is this important…and can be very powerful. It can make a major difference, if you make the effort.

Time Management

As discussed in Chapter 7, to be successful with Time Management you have to be willing to accept responsibility for your time issues. When you do this, you can make significant changes.

In addition to ideas already discussed, you might want to consider using a coach for a period of time to help you develop some time management strategies. However, if you take this step, be willing to listen carefully and be willing to accept that you probably are not doing the best job you can at managing your time. Acknowledge that you CAN make a difference.

Taking care of Yourself

Keep it simple; but make a difference. Try to do little things every day that are positive and uplifting:

> Even very short breaks, i.e. two minutes with your eyes closed, relaxed, and taking deep breaths can work wonders
>
> Exercise: do a set of pushups or some ab work; or take a couple of minutes for a short walk (without using your cell phone, PDA, or Blackberry)
>
> Treat yourself – what makes you smile? A few peanut M&Ms?
>
> Spend a couple of quality, non-work minutes with a colleague
>
> Longer breaks are wonderful and can really make a major difference to stress – a walk without the usual office

accoutrements along; a fifteen minute break (nap, snooze!); meditating on a pleasant memory is great! And so on. If you make this effort you will be amazed at how much better the rest of the day is. And, yes, you can find the time.

Take a day or two off (even an afternoon is great – go to a movie with your significant other)

A massage or spa visit

Shopping

A true exercise break, twenty minutes or longer, is great for morale and helps keep you in shape for the tough days

Spend more time with family and loved ones – a half hour with your kids playing their favorite game is an amazing tonic

Dream a little

The problem is not that we don't know what to do or that we should do it; it is that we just don't do it. We always come up with excuses, usually time-centered, that we "couldn't possibly."

Taking care of yourself is always time well spent because it does make a difference to your team and to everyone you interact with at work and in the 'real world.'

Getting help

Sometimes the smartest thing you can do when things are getting a bit overwhelming is to seek support and help. Often the best help comes from all those people you interact with regularly. Just stopping to chat with someone can be cathartic. Spending even a half hour of soul-searching time with a trusted colleague, friend, or significant other can ease many burdens. Who makes you feel good? Who brings a smile to your face? Who is a great person to bounce things off of? A great listener? Who knows just the right thing to say when you are feeling low?

Sources of support that are always worth considering:

Mentor – available through many organizations today

Coach – provided by some larger businesses; or you can

hire a personal coach

Your boss – if that works for you

A trusted colleague

Other professionals

Your friends, significant other/spouse, best buddy from years ago

> Go ahead make that call, they will be surprised and delighted to hear from you and you will wash away a lot of tension in just a few minutes chat.

Negativity

Recognizing negativity in ourselves is not something any of us relish doing; but if we are honest with who we are, it is necessary to do so in order to make changes.

Remember that:

Lowered affect – feeling down, depressed

Blaming

Complaining

Worrying

Stress, angst, upset

Etc.

Are all negative and WILL affect others.

Talk yourself UP, not D

O

W

N

We all practice self-deprecation!

Unfortunately this is the truth – we practice it so well that it becomes natural and we don't even recognize it.

> "I can't believe I screwed that up. Now I'm behind the eight ball again. What an idiot…"

> "Oh God, I've done it again. Why can't I keep my foot out of my mouth. I'm so embarrassed and I have to talk to the team again this afternoon."

This type of self-talk, and thousands of other examples, is how we consistently put ourselves down and increase our own inner (and outer) negativity. A great skill to develop is learning to catch ourselves in the act and to turn the negative into the positive.

Instead of:

> "I'm completely worthless. I've really done it this time. I'll never live this one down."

Change it to:

> "I didn't get that right, but now I know how to do it next time. I'm on top of this and I'll definitely get it next time....Come on, Koob, let's kick some butt with this next presentation."

You KNOW you are not completely worthless. And you also know, if you think about it for a second, that this will be forgotten in a very short time by everyone except perhaps you, unless you continue to berate yourself for failing.

Does this sound familiar?

> "I'm behind the eight ball again. I have so much work I will never catch up"

You probably are behind the eight ball again because you do have a lot to do. But it doesn't do you any good to reinforce the negative. Plus, you are telling yourself that you WILL never catch up. This is NOT positive reinforcement. The truth is that you do eventually get through all that work that is on your plate and move on to more work. Somehow you manage to struggle through. The key point here is that there are things you can do to alleviate some of the struggle, i.e. work some time management magic for yourself and/or find ways to take care of yourself.

One way to better take care of yourself

is to stop kicking yourself all the time!

However you typically kick yourself, you can learn to turn it around.

Negativity breeds Negativity

Positivity breeds Positivity

When it comes to how you are at work, it pays to pay attention and to make more positive choices.

Choose Wisely

Questions and Ideas for Contemplation

Spend one week self-observing to really understand the ebb and flow of your emotions, thoughts, reactions, etc. You may be surprised at how much of the time you feel stressed, worried, down, etc. Try finding brief ways to make changes – again, it is often the little things that make the most impact.

Key exercise: practice catching yourself putting yourself down – and then immediately practice turning those negative self-statements around. You might think this is a bit silly or over-the-top, but it can help. If you are a worrier, a self-doubter, and really self-critical, it can make a big difference in how you approach your work...and others at work.

PART II

Managing Difficult Employees

You will probably have to deal with a variety of employee concerns if you lead a team. If you practice the ideas and skills discussed in the first part of this book, you will have far fewer problems than otherwise, but it is wise to further develop these skills and tools for dealing with the difficult situations that can and do arise.

In this part of the book we will discuss a wide variety of concerns that you may face as a leader of people. 'Your people' will look to you for solutions. They will look to you for wisdom and they will expect you to have the tools to deal with problems expeditiously.

The good news is that all the understanding, skills, and tools discussed in the first part of this book are key to your success when dealing with difficult employee situations. When in doubt, you can always use **The Seven Keys to Understanding and Working with Difficult People**, as your foundation for success.

Self-Awareness

Self-Worth

Self-Confidence

Self-Control

Honesty

Kindness

Positivity

Chapter 19

Difficult Employees: Key Ideas

Egos are at work

Any time you have to deal with difficult behavior in others, you can be assured that people's egos are at work. Maintaining your own self-worth and self-control are critical to being successful in difficult situations. You need to bring to the table a willingness to understand the dynamics of the concern and top-notch communication skills to get to the root of the problem.

Keep in mind that as a leader and mentor another key skill you can develop is helping others develop their own sense of self-worth (See Chapter 11 and Appendix II). Most, if not all, difficult behavior is rooted in poor self-worth, poor self-image, and people's egos taking the lead in their interactions with others. Build self-confidence and self-control in your troops and they won't have to engage on the battleground of egos.

Focus on the behavior

When we can focus on the specific behaviors that are causing angst between people, we are generally much better equipped to deal successfully with the prevailing conflict. Managing a difficult employee is a much bigger challenge than focusing on a specific difficult behavior, because we tend to focus on the bad and ignore the good.

> Author's Note: In all of my work with 'difficult' people, and managers/coworkers who have had to work with difficult people, I have very rarely seen a situation that wasn't solvable. Most employees in an organization were hired because of their potential and their skills. From a practical standpoint it is typically far less expensive and time consuming to mentor a person who is having difficulties and/or get them a professional coach, than to try to fire them. And it is much less damaging to a team or

organization to deal with these concerns directly, than to pass them on to someone else's group by relocating them to another department just to 'get rid of them.'

By focusing on specific presenting behaviors, we can both mentor the individual we are concerned with and help other team members understand, as well as work with, the problem. It also gives us the opportunity to work with and build upon the strengths of an individual rather than simply zeroing in on the negative. Keep in mind that people want and need to be:

Acknowledged

Appreciated

Recognized

Rewarded

When we keep these key components in the mix, we have a much better chance of succeeding with difficult situations between employees.

What we learned

We all act and react to things, especially difficult situations, with behaviors that have served us in some way in the past. Our reactions may very well be rooted in behaviors that got us what we wanted when we were very young. A person who explodes in difficult situations may have found that throwing temper tantrums was a very useful skill when he/she was a youngster and that it still works well today. Hence he/she has continued to use what worked in the past in his/her adult life.

The key to changing learned reactions to difficulties is self-awareness. It does take time and some effort on your part and hopefully on theirs. One technique you will want to use in dealing with difficult people is to help them become aware of what they do, how it affects others, and let them know kindly, but firmly that this behavior is not acceptable at work – at least not within the framework of your team.

In other words, help them to become more self-aware of what they do and how it impacts others.

Structure

In some ways when we react to difficulties with less than ideal behaviors it is the child in us saying,

"I don't wanna."

"I'm gonna do it anyway."

"I want it my way."

"Me!"

And so on

One of the key parenting skills we need to learn when raising children is to provide structure (life parameters, life guidelines) for them. We do this for their safety and we also do it so that they learn to be successful in a structured society. Hopefully we also teach them creativity and the joy of discovery as well, but we DO have to set limits.

> Here is an interesting sidebar: I have found that often parents who complain about having difficult, uncontrolled children were very poor at setting parameters, structure, guidelines for their children to follow and/or very poor at consistently enforcing those parameters.

In working with people who are using less-than ideal-behaviors at work, a key technique we can develop is helping them set parameters and guidelines that are acceptable to everyone. Primarily we do that by setting an example and by letting everyone know what our work values are. We can also do this more specifically and demonstratively when the situation calls for it.

As an example:

> We may set the stage for our team by encouraging openness and honesty in everything we do, as well as with everyone with whom we interact. We broadcast this through our own actions and by talking the talk – telling people on a regular basis that these are qualities we value.

> If we have an employee who is regularly using deception and behind-the-back behaviors to get what he/she wants, we may find it necessary to let them know kindly but

firmly that these behaviors are unacceptable. We will need to find ways to let them know very specifically that underhanded behaviors are not an acceptable means of working with people. How we do this and what parameters we set will be based on the degree of the concern and whether or not the individual is getting the message. For example: on one level we would make an effort to reward more positive, open behaviors, but if things don't improve we might also let them know that continuing concerns in this arena could affect their recognition, evaluation, opportunities for advancement, etc.

Setting guidelines and parameters at work can be a juggling act. On the one hand you want to make sure that concerns are being addressed. You also want to make sure you are setting the same standards for everyone and not just focusing on one person. Be judicious and work positivity into the mix whenever possible – acknowledgment, appreciation, recognition, and reward – as your fundamental approach. But be willing to deal with concerns directly when you need to. Reinforce the positive; be willing to nip negativity in the bud.

Don't forget to let everyone know that when you set parameters that these are basic guidelines, and that you support open discussion on all issues, innovation, and creativity.

Bring things out in the open

Many times difficult problems occur at work because people don't understand the full ramifications of any given situation. One of our key jobs as a mentor of our team players is to help people communicate effectively. It can be difficult in situations that have festered for long periods of time to get people to open up, especially when there is a great deal of whining, complaining, blaming, finger-pointing. etc., going on behind the scenes. But it IS possible. It is ESSENTIAL, if you wish to get everyone back on the same page, working effectively together.

We will discuss techniques for working in and opening up a variety of difficult situations, and how to work this type of magic with a wide range of difficult behavior patterns. However, keep in mind that every situation is different and you have to learn to use a creative approach to handling what comes your way. We can provide the understanding, skills, and tools for you to use; it is your task as a manager and leader of people to be successful by being open and flexible to the possibilities of the current situation you are dealing with.

People are different

By far the most common reason people have difficulties with other people is because we all see the world differently. Sometimes differences in opinion or perspective can, over time, create tremendous chasms between individuals and teams. Getting people to open up and talk about differences is an important skill you can develop to help mitigate these types of challenges.

Keep this key concept in mind in any difficult situation you have to deal with. Somehow and 'some-when' it is highly likely that the people involved rubbed each other the wrong way because of differences in how they looked at or approached something. Getting to the root cause of difficulties between people is one of the keys to being successful with them.

Over-the-top communication skills

Good communication skills are fundamental to good management. Great communication skills are essential to great leadership. 'Over-the-top' communication means going that extra mile to learn how to mentor, draw people out, open things up, and get your people talking with each other – which, as you know, in some difficult situations can be very hard to do.

Listening is your best tool

By far the best skill we can develop is to be an engaged listener. Listening and hearing what others feel is important to understanding their concerns and it shows acknowledgement and appreciation. It helps recognize what someone else is imparting as important. Even if you don't agree, it shows respect for them by showing you are willing to take the time to understand and consider their side of things.

[The next chapter focuses on the key basic and 'over-the-top' communication tools you need to be successful in difficult situations.]

Learn to Ask

Asking opens up many doors. Keep this key communication tool handy whenever you are dealing with difficult situations. It is far better than demanding, complaining, blaming, directing, etc. And while you may have the right to use these 'tools' as a boss, you will probably have considerable difficulty in managing people concerns. And you and your people are not going to enjoy work much.

Most difficult people do not know they are being Difficult

This is hard to believe sometimes, but it is true. Even really difficult people, i.e. people that almost everyone else sees as difficult, rarely see themselves in that light. Typically they see themselves as generally likeable and everyone else as difficult!

It is all about perspective. We all see the world differently. As a boss and mentor we have to consistently remind ourselves that logic, what may seem obvious to us, even what is 'real' or 'true' to most people, may not be what a 'difficult' person sees. Understanding their perspective through focused listening gives you the knowledge you need to begin to deal with the situation.

There are two (or more) sides to every argument. AND, a very key point – one side may not be more 'right' than another. Being right almost always has to do with ego and very rarely has to do with actually needing to be right. By far the majority of situations in which people are insisting that they are right (95%?) have moved far away from what is important to petty issues ruled by ego.

Part of your task as a leader is to move people out from the importance of clinging to 'rightness' to doing what is best for the team and organization. Help people to be right, by acknowledging them, appreciating them, recognizing them, and rewarding them. Help them 'be right' for the organization by getting them to acknowledge what is best for the team.

Difficulty IS in the eyes of the beholder. As a leader it is always important to work with all sides of a difficult situation. Our definition for a difficult person is "Anyone who causes anyone else angst." In any difficult situation that is usually all involved parties. By maintaining your own self-awareness, self-worth, self-confidence, and self-control you can step outside that ring and begin to bring equanimity to the proceedings.

If they do know they are being difficult, they may be too upset to care.

Emotions play a huge role in difficult situations and part of your job may be to calm people down and get them all on a level playing field. That is all about great communication, understanding, and getting people to open up and talk about what is upsetting them.

Keep in mind that negativity and difficulty is typically rooted in fear.

> Fear of loss
>
> Fear of being thought less of
>
> Fear of being less than
>
> Fear of not being good enough
>
> Fear of failure
>
> And so on.

Help people move from fear to understanding and you have solved much of the problem.

Difficult people are getting a reward for their behavior

Difficult behavior is learned. A presenting behavior may be a technique someone has used since they were a child to get their way. We tend to use what has worked for us in the past and as long as it continues to work we will continue to use it more or less effectively (depending on your perspective!). The motive for discontinuing the behavior comes from people not reacting in the ways that the difficult person expects. When the difficult behavior is not reinforced; it will disappear.

> Take away the reward and the behavior is likely to change.

This is another key idea that is worth keeping in the back of your mind when dealing with any difficult situation. People react; the situation escalates. Lead by example. Take the typical reinforcement of the behavior out of the sequence and it is the start toward changing the dynamics of that concern.

You can only change yourself; you cannot change other people...

As a leader this important key to "Understanding and Working with Difficult People," is something you will want to impart to others. When they understand this, they can learn to adjust their own approach in difficult situations rather than continuing to beat their heads against a wall by using the same old tried and hardly true methods they have continued to use with their difficult person.

I often add the word 'directly' to the end of this statement –

> "You can only change yourself;
>
> you cannot change other people...directly."

Because when we change our behavior, i.e. our reactions to a difficult person's behaviors, to in-control responses, their behavior is likely to change toward us.

Find out what the difficult person wants, needs and cares about

The basic act of trying to understand a person changes the dynamics of a difficult situation and sets a completely different stage. People tend to be much more willing to compromise and even to make significant life changes when they have had a chance to tell their side of the story. A key skill for leaders dealing with difficulties is to learn to draw out people through open, honest, kind, and compassionate communications.

After all, Kind-frontation is so much better than Confrontation. (see Crowe, "Carefrontation")

And in the final analysis -- DOCUMENT!

It is especially important to document everything important when you are working through difficult situations at work. You can never be completely sure what direction something might take so be sure to keep careful notes of meetings, mediations, e-mails, memos, etc. You may also want the people involved to put things in writing whenever you feel it might be important. It is better to be safe.

Take notes on:

> Who
>
> What
>
> When
>
> How
>
> How much
>
> Where
>
> Why
>
> And so on

Keep confidential information in a safe place. You might be surprised at who has access to your files and computer information.

> Author's Note: I once had an employee whose wife was above me, albeit indirectly, in the chain of command. I found out the hard way that he had access to her keys, which opened all the doors in our building. He was entering my office at night and stealing confidential files on fellow employees that he would use as leverage against them. I found out about it because he made the mistake of trying to leverage me with information he had stolen.

If there is any doubt, make sure confidential files are safely stored and protected from prying eyes.

Questions and Ideas for Contemplation

The key ideas in this chapter are the fundamental concepts that can help us make wiser choices when working through difficult people concerns. Keep these in mind as you read the rest of this book; they will help you begin to develop personal strategies for dealing with situations that may arise at work.

A useful tool might be to create a card with these key concepts and to keep it handy for an occasional reminder while at work. Or copy what is below, laminate it, and stick it in your wallet or by your desk.

Key Concepts for Being Successful with Difficult Employees

Egos are at work

Focus on their behavior

We react with behaviors that have served us in the past

Bring things out in the open

People are different – it is the most common cause of angst between others

Provide structure/guidelines

Use Over-the-top communications

Listening is your best tool

Learn to ask

Emotions play a major role

They are getting a reward for their behavior

You can only change yourself; you cannot change other people...directly

Find out what they want, need, and care about

Document

Chapter 20

Communicating in Difficult Situations

"...difficult people become even more difficult when they are

misunderstood" (Bell and Smith)

or perceive to be misunderstood (Koob).

People want to be heard; they want to be able to express their concerns, what is important to them, and their needs. The more you can offer them the opportunity to do this the easier your task will be to mitigate difficulties that arise in your work environment.

As a leader you have developed some good communication skills; however, it is worth mentioning some of the skills and tools you probably already use in order to give some insight in using these in difficult situations. As we discuss more specific difficult behaviors throughout the rest of this book, we will offer additional suggestions on using key communication techniques.

Important

The purpose of this chapter is two-fold:

> To give you an understanding of techniques that work in difficult situations

> To provide information that you can pass on to team members so they have the skills and tools they need to be successful when they find themselves engaged in a difficult interaction

Training team members is a great concept that we often don't always take full advantage of. Not only can this ease our burden when leading a team, but it is another means of preventive maintenance – when people understand key ideas about

"Understanding and Working with Difficult People" they are more likely to apply them throughout their lives. [My book, *Succeeding with Difficult Coworkers* focuses on the dynamics of people on more or less the same level within a team.]

Open the door

Whether a person is ranting about some issue or another, or moody, reserved, and unwilling to engage, the best strategy you can have is to give them the space and time to let it out. By focusing on them and listening carefully, you open the door in a variety of ways:

> You provide an opportunity for them to communicate their concerns to you
>
> You acknowledge who they are and their desires
>
> You disengage any immediate difficulties
>
> You set a different stage and different dynamics for future interactions
>
> You develop a deeper understanding of this person/your personnel/your people
>
> You create an opportunity and atmosphere where learning and understanding can take place

Listening Skills

> "Listen without judgment"
>
> (Perkins)

Listening is your best skill. The following are key ideas that work in difficult situations. Many difficult concerns can be dealt with quickly when you use these types of techniques to understand what is driving the difficult behavior:

Gain their attention

If someone is ranting and raving; let them wind down by showing focus and an intent to listen. Repeat their name several times, if necessary, to gain their attention.

> "Steve, Steve,...Steve, I'm listening. Please tell me what is bothering you. I want to understand what you need me to do for you...."

It may take some patience, but let them cool off enough so you can help them get out of their negative stuff. Then you can find out what the concern is. Once they have calmed, it is typically best to move them to a neutral location so you can focus exclusively on what they need to get off their chest. If several people are involved, it is often best to get them separated and spend time with each before bringing them together to work toward a solution.

If the person is passive and uncommunicative, you have to be very patient and draw them out. A neutral location, that will help them to feel safe, is essential – usually their space is better than your office. You can allow them to choose the location. A walk outside might feel safer to them than any space in the office. Let them know they are free and safe to communicate with you.

> "Nan, I know you are upset about something and I want to help. Let's sit down and chat about what you really need. I'm here for you and I want you to feel comfortable and happy in your job...."

You may have to gently cajole them before they will open up; once they do start sharing, keep them going by being supportive and encouraging.

It is important not to show any signs of frustration or impatience with a reserved and reticent person. They will take this personally and clam up even more.

Focus on them

Your demeanor and focus tells another person 'where you are/who you are.' When dealing with a difficult person you need to use eye contact and body language that says, "I'm here for you," "I'm focusing on everything you are telling me." You also need to use verbal and physical cues that are encouraging and supportive.

Eye contact

Try to engage them at a safe distance for them – they will let you know what that is, because they will back away if you get too close. Maintain as much eye contact as is comfortable for them.

Some people may engage you, others may shy away. It is important, however, to stay focused on them. If they are not comfortable with direct eye contact, then focus more generally on their face, and only occasionally try to make eye contact. The more comfortable and safe they feel the more they will engage you, so stay on top of this throughout the discussion.

Posture

Keep a relaxed, non-threatening posture. Be self-confident without showing any aggression. It may help to mimic their general posture, i.e. if they are sitting, sit; if they are standing, stand relaxed and maintain a safe, non-aggressive position. Hint: Don't mimic such things as slouching, rigidity, etc. You want to create a safe environment for them.

Gestures

Use gestures to your advantage. Simple (and slow) hand gestures, nods, shrugs, etc. can let a person know you are listening carefully to what they are saying. Overly demonstrative gestures may get in the way, or appear threatening, so try to judge how what you are doing is being taken.

Verbal cues

Short, encouraging vocal cues are very important to letting someone know they have your full attention:

> "Yes,"

> "I understand,"

> "Uh huh,"

> "Good,"

> "Thanks,"

> "I see,"

> "Go on."

> And so on.

Silence

Often just remaining quiet, even during pregnant pauses, is the best policy for drawing someone out. This is especially important with a person who is reserved and shy. Give them time to open up. Pauses in proceedings give a person time to get their thoughts together. In other words, don't jump in just because they have stopped, wait a few seconds, and then, if you deem it appropriate, paraphrase something they just said or ask a probing, open-ended question to stimulate further discussion.

Paraphrasing

A key listening skill is following up important details with a response that shows that you are listening and that you understand. This also opens the door to see if you have understood them correctly and gives the person an opportunity to give you feed back on whether you have got it right.

> "What I'm hearing you say, Paul, is that you feel Ralph is ignoring all of your input on the Bosworth project and claiming you haven't done anything. Is that right?"

> "I think I understand what you are telling me, Stacy. You feel Henry is saying things behind your back that are untrue. Could you give me some specific examples so I can understand exactly what is going on?"

You don't have to agree with them; just let them know you understand what they have said. When you are juggling different, and often conflicting, perspectives from employees, it is important not to offer any judgments or take any sides. You may have to deal with this later through some sort of mediation between several people, but right now you are simply seeking understanding of what the difficulty is.

Ask

Asking questions shows interest and commitment to understand. It acknowledges someone and what they are trying to impart to you. It also gives you the opportunity to take this to a deeper level and really find out what the dynamics of the concern are.

> As an example: though the presenting problem may be that Paul feels that Ralph is ignoring his input, it is very likely that he and Ralph have a history of concerns and this is an opportunity to understand the dynamics of this by further

probing. The other side of the coin might be that Ralph really feels that Paul isn't contributing very much to the project and is frustrated because he thinks he is doing all the work. The truth may lie somewhere in-between.

When you do ask questions, avoid 'why,' it is often seen as accusatory.

> "I understand that you feel Ralph is being unfair about your work on the Bosworth project. Why do you feel this way?"

This may seem like an innocuous question to ask, but if you are Paul and strongly emotionally involved, it may feel like you are questioning his right to feel the way he does.

> Better: "Paul, I understand that you feel Ralph is being unfair about your contributions to the Bosworth project. Can you tell me a little more about some of ideas that you wanted included and the discussions you had with Ralph about these?"

Apologize

Not necessarily for anything you did. Use it as a tool to gain their attention so that they focus on you, and to let them know you are with them:

> "Francis, I'm sorry you are upset. I am here to help. Let's talk this out, okay?"

Give them time

Typically most of us want to jump right on the bandwagon and solve things. When listening to someone who has significant concerns, it is important to make sure they have had their say – their full say – before offering suggestions, solutions, mediation, etc. Resist the urge to jump in and offer advice. And most importantly, don't make judgments. Stay neutral and open. Taking care to stay on top of your personal reactions can be very important. A 'difficult person,' or simply someone who is currently very upset, may take even innocuous gestures or statements negatively.

That is why gentle probing with open-ended questions can help you get to the heart of the matter. The current issue may be the tip of the iceberg.

You can always ask them if they have anything else to add. Several great techniques are to:

> Ask if they want to say/include anything else
>
> Paraphrase/summarize what you have heard and ask if you have understood and whether they want to add anything
>
> Probe a little deeper by asking questions about key points
>
> Set another time with them so they can add anything they may have forgotten

Seek specificity

Whenever possible, without interrupting their flow, and when you feel you need to understand something better, be willing to ask.

Take notes

While it may not be feasible or even comfortable for you, a good listening technique is to ask them if they mind your taking written notes of key points. This can show that you are serious about their concern and that you intend to follow-up. Be careful with this technique as some people might find it suspicious; that is why asking them for permission to do so is the best approach.

> "Wayne, I can see you have a lot to tell me, and I want to make sure I get everything right so I can help you out. Would you mind if I jotted down a few of your key points while we chat?"

Your demeanor is key

Be sure to be: friendly, kind, open, and honest. Show compassion, if appropriate, for difficult concerns. Adding humanness to the proceedings can help someone feel like you are there for them.

Feelings

Acknowledge their feelings and let them know that how they feel is important to you

> "Carole, I can see you are upset about this issue. I want

135

you to know I am here for you and I will make every effort to help you through this."

"I am sorry you feel so unappreciated by some of the members of the team, Mark. I want you to know that I want to understand how you feel and also let you know that I am here to help. Let's work through this together. Okay?"

Summarize

Even if you have done this several times throughout the conversation, it is best to follow-up at the end with another summary. It helps to ensure that you got everything that is important right the first time, and it further acknowledges the person and what they said.

Thank them

This is a great ending choice that shows that what they have shared is important. It also helps to set the stage for any further discussions around this concern with this person.

"Thanks Jean. I really appreciate your willingness to share these difficult feelings and ideas with me. I know it wasn't easy for you. I will follow through with this and you can count on my support."

Beyond listening - responding

"Respond without blame"

(Koob)

All of the techniques described above continue to apply throughout your discussion with someone. When you do have the opportunity to begin to ask more in-depth questions and to take the discussion a step further, keep in mind that your goal is still to comprehend what the issues are. Even if you want to take some time now to offer solutions or suggestions, do so with the idea that you may have a good bit more to listen to and understand.

The information you gather is the catalyst for what follows. Often you will have to take a step back, engage other people, and draw together interested parties before offering responses to concerns. Make sure you let the people you talk to know that you have taken them seriously and that you will seek the best possible solution for them, the team, and the organization.

Solutions are not always cut-and-dried, and you certainly do not want to buy into office politics or petty squabbles. However, by listening carefully you now have an understanding that will help you make the best possible decisions for your team. You also have prepared the ground for better interpersonal dynamics throughout your team by letting people get things off their chests. Sometimes that is as beneficial as anything else you can do, or any solutions you can come up with.

Pay attention to what you say and How you say it

Difficult situations often require a great deal of sensitivity and finesse. Stay on top of how you are coming across. Watch for the other person's body language to give you cues on how they are reacting to what you say. Try to stay neutral, open and non-threatening.

Remember, there are always positive ways to phrase things, ask questions, and explore solutions.

Ask them for their solution

Though it may surprise you at times, people (even difficult people) are often fairly judicious about suggesting solutions to concerns. While you may get a, "Yeah, fire the jerk," you also may get some intelligent ideas on possible approaches,"

> "If we could just move our desks slightly, the lighting problem would be resolved. I don't think George would have a problem with that if you were willing to broach the subject. He just always seems so reticent about things if I bring them up. It's like he sees everything as a power struggle. All I want to do is get along."

Learn from them

You can learn a great deal from difficult situations.

> You can learn specific techniques that work best for you

137

You can learn what is driving/motivating people in your office

You can learn a good bit about leading people

You can learn a tremendous amount about yourself

You can learn to be a better manager and leader

Mediation, compromising, mentoring, coaching

Listening gives you the understanding to move forward with personnel concerns and potential solutions. You may want to get opposing parties together for a frank discussion. You will probably, on occasion, have to mediate disputes and offer compromise solutions. You will also want to mentor and coach key personnel so that what is now out on the table remains something that can be talked about and dealt with.

Often people on teams have long histories of interpersonal conflict. You are not necessarily going to change that overnight. But by keeping things open, and by helping people talk about concerns, you are setting the stage for change and giving them a venue to sound off in as they get used to how you expect things to be handled on your team – openly and honestly.

Never put yourself or anyone else at risk!

It is very rare that concerns at work get volatile, but it is always important to work from a **safety first** perspective. If you ever feel a situation might get out of hand, get help immediately and make every effort to neutralize the volatility quickly. Often just repeating a person's name and letting them know you are there for them will work. However, remove yourself and others from the situation if at all possible if there is any question about what might happen.

Calling in help from another appropriate venue at work may be the smart call if you have any trepidation at all about a person or situation. Know ahead of time where and to whom you can go if you need to.

Questions and Ideas for Contemplation

By practicing your listening and communication skills you can be very successful at resolving disputes that arise at work. One of the key things you accomplish through developing and using these skills is a more open and honest work environment, which will help minimize difficulties that may arise and will create an atmosphere in which solutions are more readily attained.

Even if you are new to a leadership role, or taking over a team that has a history of interpersonal conflicts, you can make a difference. It is called 'on-the-job-training.' The key is self-awareness. Then it is a matter of knowing the skills and tools that can make a difference and trying them out in the field.

Keep in mind that your communication skills and leadership are the exemplar that your employees see every day. How you go about working through concerns and disputes will be noticed and it will make a difference in how other people work together.

Chapter 21

Moody, Depressed

Negative affect can rub off very quickly in an office environment. However, you have a valuable skill and tool available that can make a major difference with moody, 'down' team members if used consistently and persistently – positivity.

Hands down positivity can and will work wonders. Here is a little story I like to tell that illustrates this from both sides of the coin:

> You probably couldn't be feeling much more beat up and down than I was the day following my sinus surgery. My sinuses were packed with gauze, I was miserable, and I needed to go to the store to pick up some items to make it through the next couple of days. On top of that my boss was already pressuring me to come back to work, even though it had only been twelve hours since I had left the operating table. I was not a happy camper.
>
> I went into the grocery store near my house and luckily my favorite checkout clerk was on duty. After garnering what I needed, I chose her line because I knew this bubbly, outgoing, grandmotherly-type was just the tonic I needed. As she began to check my items through, she immediately noticed my condition and asked me in a concerned way what was wrong. Then she kindly and amiably chatted with me. Even though I was feeling miserable physically and psychologically down, she was easily able to lift my spirits with her kind, compassionate, friendly words. I felt a great deal better leaving the store than when I came in.
>
> A few days later, feeling much better but still recovering, I went to the same store and was able to go through the same lady's line. Once again, her positive chatter lightened my day. She asked me how I was doing, having remembered how sick I had felt a few days earlier, and

told me how much better I looked, and so on. It was another pleasant encounter that boosted my spirits even more.

Perhaps a week after that, I went back to the same store, saw her at one of the checkout counters, and smiled. After getting what I needed, I picked up a bouquet of flowers near the checkout and went in her line. After ringing up my items she handed the flowers to me. I handed the bouquet back to her and said, "These are for you, for being so nice to me." She stood there with the flowers in hand, a big tear ran down her cheek, and then she shuffled around the counter and gave me a big grandmotherly hug.

That is positivity in action – it only costs a little bit of effort and it can make all the difference in the world. When you get other people on board the positivity bandwagon and involved in kindness to others it WILL make a major difference at work. You may not entirely change a person's outlook on life, but you can make a difference in how they feel and how they are at work.

The best tools you have

Team members

Great leaders make use of every resource available to them. Every member of your team is a potential gold mine when working through difficult situations. You have to be wise and judicious in what you choose, but communications training, motivational seminars, etc. can help make other team members become positive catalysts that can aid your own mentoring work. Not only can this add considerable impact to what you are trying to do, it can save you time and money. Plus it helps build responsibility and trains other employees in key leadership and mentoring skills.

Spending some time and money on training key team members (or your entire team) can pay major dividends over time. You will find that people will step up to the plate time and again to help out when things get tough.

Team players are also an excellent source of positive ideas that can affect general office attitude, productivity, and quality control. Don't be hesitant to ask what will make your people happy. They will very likely come up with some great and inexpensive ways to add to the positivity mix. Making use of these key 'tools' is wise leadership.

Key skills revisited

This is a good time to revisit some key ideas discussed earlier (See Chapter 17), with the emphasis now placed on working with difficult people and through difficult situations.

Acknowledgment

With our very busy work lives we often run from meeting to meeting and task to task. People, our people, unfortunately often don't get the attention they deserve and NEED from us or from other managers. The simple act of letting someone know they are alive and valued can have a major impact on their outlook. It really doesn't take a lot of time for you to:

> Say "hello" to a team member who is struggling

> Send a one or two-line e-mail saying something positive – "Anne, hope your day is going well. Let me know if you need anything."

> Give someone a thumbs-up as you make that extra effort to pass their work station

> Stopping in a cubicle just to give someone who is down a quick compliment

> Etc.

Hint: Be sure to get other team members on board this A-train. People like and want to help. When you enlist additional aid, you help yourself and you help your team. It feels good to be nice, to be kind and it spreads the wealth around.

It is all about making the effort to say, "I know you are here, and you ARE important." Let them know that they matter. These small things CAN help change a person's work life around.

Appreciation

Acknowledgement is a form of appreciation, but you can go a little bit further with one of the most basic and best tools there is – saying 'thank you.' Use this great tool with your entire team on a regular basis. It is one thing that doesn't ever get old and when sincerely given, is always appreciated. It can help make the mundane special AND it is positive reinforcement that says very specifically, "Do this again. I like this behavior."

> "Barb, I want to thank you for getting that data to me on time. It really helps out my schedule."

> "Thanks Zack, your insight into the Steven's contract has got me thinking. I'll let you know what I come up with. Keep those creative juices flowing."

> "Ollie, I got your note. Thanks. I will keep this on the front burner."

> "Sven, I appreciate your positive comment to Barb this afternoon at the meeting. I know she appreciated it too." (Always make an effort to reinforce the positive behaviors you see in someone who tends to be moody and depressed.)

Thanking is a great training tool. When you reinforce the positive things people do and say, everyone affected and within earshot will remember and want to repeat that behavior. It feels good to get kudos. When you are dealing with negativity, find every angle you can to encourage the positive. You may have to stretch things a bit at first and thank someone for very small wins, but if you stick to your positivity/appreciation program you will make an impact and positive behaviors will increase throughout your team.

Appreciation can be shown in a variety of ways:

> Smiles

> Compliments – we can always offer more of these

> Kind words

> Small gifts, flowers, etc. for work well done

Author's Note: There are many things you can do to appreciate "your people." Here is one that worked for me,

> I made sure I recognized everyone's birthday. I would get flowers or take each of my employees to lunch on or about their birthday. Since I had a manageable team size (about twenty) this was an inexpensive, positive way to say "you

matter,' and 'thanks.' For larger teams you might simply send a card and give the person a call.

These little things matter – a lot!

Be sure to spread the wealth around and appreciate everyone. You can avoid playing favorites by making sure you emphasize the positive with all your team players. However, people who are down and generally negative might need a bit more attention to start with.

Brainstorm ways that work for you and your team and that fit into your organization's culture.

Acknowledgment and Appreciation can be extremely effective when used consistently. When you make this part of your overall leadership style, people will notice, and you will notice the positive results.

Recognition

Recognition is taking appreciation a step further. It raises the bar just a bit by including others in the process.

> Memo sent to entire team: "I want to thank Ed for his fine work on the Holden papers. You all know how important this effort has been to our team's success this month so please give him a hearty pat on the back."

> At a meeting: "I want to recognize Ionia, Bob, and Ralph for their hard work on the Gregory contract. It is in final review and we will be kicking it upstairs later this week. Kudos everyone."

> "We are going to have a small get-together in the coffee room at four to thank everyone for their efforts on getting this prototype off the drawing board and into production. Eats and treats. Thanks everyone for making this happen."

Again, it is important to spread the wealth around, but try to include people who are struggling in the loop whenever possible. Recognizing people can have an important impact on how they perceive their life and work.

The great thing about acknowledgment, appreciation, and recognition is that it is difficult to overdo it. It is immediate, people feel good, and life moves on – usually with just that little bit of extra spring in the step and perhaps a small smile on the inside.

Reward

Rewards tend to be more formal. Organizations typically have in-house reward systems – bonuses, recommendations, certificates, etc. A wise leader makes sure he/she uses these to the utmost benefit of team members. Hint: When appropriate, it is advisable to encourage your employees to apply for specific reward programs that they may not be eligible for unless they make the effort to enroll.

You can take rewards a step further by developing team-based and success/effort-based recognitions. Again, these don't have to be expensive, nor should they involve extensive forms, processes, or effort to accomplish.

Keep them simple and do not overdo it. Reward can be overused. Typically, however, we all tend to be too busy and don't reward people enough for their hard work. Use reward judiciously as an extension and more powerful type of recognition.

Important: formal organization-wide reward programs -- bonuses are a good example – tend to lack impact because they have become ingrained into the culture and are expected. Many times they have lost almost all the ability to inspire and motivate and, if anything, tend to be somewhat demoralizing for the vast majority of employees. That is why team-based recognition and reward can be powerful motivators.

> They are more immediate – they respond to something that has or is happening
>
> Colleagues and friends share in the success
>
> People have something tangible that says, "I did a good job."

Simple things are often the best: certificates, plaques, small prizes. Believe it or not the larger the reward the less it tends to work as a motivator and the more problems (jealousy, in-fighting, de-moralization) happen as a result.

Try to make sure that opportunities exist for everyone to succeed and reap the benefits of recognition and reward programs. Spread the wealth around whenever feasible.

Spread it Around

Acknowledgement, Appreciation, Recognition, and Reward are good for everyone if used consistently and judiciously. You will find that these are great techniques to use with all 'difficult types.' But always keep in mind that everyone appreciates being appreciated. Unfortunately, when things are going well, we often forget to thank people for who they are and what they are doing. Make these techniques a habit.

> Author's Note: I was once the Administrative Dean of a summer program. The job mostly consisted of keeping things humming, i.e. taking care of logistical concerns. I applied myself diligently and enjoyed the position, but I wasn't aware of how the job was impacting me until one day when I was standing with the camp director looking over the flow of campers heading to lunch, he casually mentioned that he appreciated my good work. It was the first recognition of any kind that I had received. It was as if a considerable amount of held-in tension washed immediately from my body. I thought (and hoped) I was doing a good job. Even though I had not had any negative feedback, I had not had any positive feedback either for those first four weeks. That simple statement of appreciation made a BIG difference and I was able to relax and enjoy the rest of the summer because I knew I was making a positive difference.

Work at it if you have to

Sometimes with employees who are extremely moody and down (or whiney and complaining – see next chapter), you have to make a bit of effort to find things to appreciate and recognize. Make the effort. The more you reinforce the small positives you can find, the better success you will have and the more they will make an effort to get other kudos from you. It may be basic psychology, but it works.

We all have our moments

We all have good and bad days. Most of us are rarely 'UP' all the time. As a leader it is your responsibility to keep a finger on the pulse of your team and team members, and recognize when a little bit of extra attention and appreciation might be in order. Making this effort and taking some time to stay on top of things can save you major headaches later on. When in doubt, ask:

> "Don, you seem a bit under the weather today. Anything I can do to help?"

> "Tough week, Nancy? I know this job change has been hard on you. Do you want to talk about it?"

Serious Depression

It is possible that someone in your group may be suffering from clinical depression or another serious problem. You can look for clues, but diagnosing and attempting to treat a person who has serious medical or psychological concerns is probably beyond your training and responsibility. If you have a reason to feel this is a significant problem, please help them to get help. Be judicious about what you say to them and how you go about offering help. Consult with your Human Resources department and/or other appropriate organizational departments to understand proper processes and procedures to deal with these types of concerns.

Questions and Ideas for Contemplation

You never really know the full extent of the problems that someone is dealing with on a regular basis. As a leader you make a difference by helping when and how you can. You want to encourage and support without being intrusive and sometimes you do have to walk a fine line. When in doubt, simple positive gestures and expressions of appreciation can matter the most.

Keep in mind, and share this with helpful team members, that this must be an ongoing endeavor. Positivity can work wonders, but any negativity may put a damper on the effort you are making. Be consistent and be persistent.

Chapter 22

Whining, Complaining, and General Negativity

You have seen this type many times, and there really does seem to be one in every bunch. Unfortunately they can have a marked negative impact on the general mood of a team or department. Their doom and gloom approach to their work can drag down everyone they come in contact with. They can't seem to see anything from a positive perspective. Often we wish we could just help them see that there is a better way to look at life.

> "Come on Dave, things really aren't so bad around here. As a matter of fact, this is a great place to work. Snap out of it buddy. Look at the bright side...."

The truth is...

You can't change other people...

Directly.

However,

You (AND your team members) have a great many skills and tools available to make a difference over time. It is important to remember that your goal is not to change this person's general outlook on life – though that would be great if it eventually happened – but to effect positive change within your team and office. Hopefully you will make a positive difference to them, but that goal is far beyond your leadership role.

> Note: Serious personnel concerns may need to be addressed through other appropriate venues at work. Counseling and medical issues need to be dealt with at a professional level. As a leader sometimes you need to make hard decisions about whether personal issues have

reached a stage where they need to be addressed further, outside the scope of your role, by trained professionals. Never put yourself or any team member at risk. When in doubt, seek help.

Work the Magic

In the face of persistent positivity, negativity usually doesn't stand a chance. I have seen this time and time again in work and life situations. The hard part is that when you are working with someone who is generally negative, it is, in a sense, their life-style, their approach to the world. You need to be willing to keep up your positive efforts with them in spite of how negatively they approach their work and regardless of what they say and do. It does take time, but you can make a major difference in your relationship with them, and quite possibly in their overall demeanor at work.

Humor

Good old-fashioned fun and goofing around can be a part of your repertoire also, if you are comfortable with that while being a boss. Adding some laughter to your life, and theirs, can help dissipate a moody, or even tense, atmosphere. Using humor judiciously will help you appear more human, too. Another big positive in the stressful business world of today.

Winning small

A key point of this chapter is that **simple**, **small**, and **often** are key ideas. Particularly when working with someone who is struggling with and/or against work (and quite likely, their life). You will be much more likely to succeed if you keep up a positive program with them over an extended period of time. Getting other members of your team on this bandwagon can have a critical impact as well.

Seeking Attention

A whiner or complainer may be seeking attention. Unfortunately they have learned that negative behaviors have often gotten them what they want. The simple and wise solution is to give them positive attention – acknowledgment, appreciation, recognition – AND to avoid buying into their negativity.

Regular positive contact with a person who tends to focus on the negative will often help dissipate a good bit of their tendency to verbalize their discontent. The best strategy is frequent small gestures of goodwill and positivity. Keep this program up and enlist the help of other team members and you will very likely see some changes taking place.

Ask

Sometimes all it takes to make a difference is to ask a person who is struggling at work what will help:

> Ask specifically about issues they raise (see below)
>
> Ask them what will help them enjoy their work life more
>
> Ask them what ideas they have and what changes they would make

You may or may not get answers that will help you work toward positive solutions to their concerns. But you will find out a good bit more about what is driving their discontent. Sometimes you may find that solutions are simple; at other times it may be that this person has a negative outlook on just about everything and the solution is not so much about fixing something as about working with them toward a more positive outlook at work.

What Problems? What Solutions?

When asked to delineate what is troubling them, whiners and complainers will often sidestep. Part of being successful with them is to bring their concerns out in the open.

> "John, I notice you seem to be unhappy with the work on the Stevens proposal. Could you specify what is troubling you, so we can consider changes?"
>
> "I just don't think Bob is doing a very good job.... mumble, mumble, mumble..."
>
> "Okay. So let's sit down in my office at 4:30 and go through the proposal piecemeal and you can help me understand how you would make it better."
>
> "Well, I'm kind of busy...ah...maybe you should talk with Bob. I'm not sure..."

> "John, I want your input. I'll see you at 4:30. Bring the proposal with your notes and we'll knock this out together."

Being firm and insistent, but avoiding negativity may be strategies you will need to use with this type of personality. You may find, and this is quite common, that John has a personal problem with Bob and is using the Stevens proposal as a means to vent. [See also Chapter 23 on Mediation] By insisting on bringing John's whining and complaining to a head, you are stating that:

> Complaining and whining behaviors will not go unnoticed, nor will they be put up with

> You have a handle on what is happening in the office and how people feel

> You will take action about legitimate concerns that arise

Do this several times and John will quickly understand that you are not going to let pervasive negativity slide. Typically in the future he will think long and hard about raising issues that don't have any substance.

Important: You can use this type of approach without negativity on your part. Yes, you will probably need to be direct, firm, and insistent, but stay within your self-worth by being calm and in-control. Whenever possible get some positivity into the mix:

> Thank John for being willing to be open about his concerns.

> Offer appreciation if he seems to make some progress toward a more positive approach

> And so on.

Help them find Solutions

One of the best techniques to use with whiners and complainers is to put the onus on them to seek out the best possible solutions to their concerns. As suggested above, simply bringing the concern out in the open may have a dramatic impact on what and how much they continue to verbalize to anyone and everyone. Taking this a step further and having them work through their concerns, and having them make an effort to suggest possible solutions can have some very positive ramifications:

> It takes the onus off you or someone else to work on this

> It helps them become more responsible for their work environment and enjoyment

> It gives them a feeling of control and power, without taking anything away from anyone else

> It can help build responsibility and character as a potential future leader

> You may find that they have good ideas that will positively impact the success of your team

You probably shouldn't give them carte blanche, but by getting them to work toward possible solutions you set the stage for intelligent discussions amongst team members on specific issues.

> "John, I understand a bit better some of the things you feel are not quite right with the contract. How about bringing me a list of changes you would make that you feel would improve things. Be sure to address all of your concerns. I expect this on my desk by tomorrow afternoon. Thanks. I know you will do a great job."

This places the solution to John's concern right back into his hands. It is very likely that he will not be very happy about having to deal with his complaining in a productive way. You may get some inspired work out of him, or not. What **will** happen is that John will understand very clearly that he better be ready for the consequences if he is going to whine, complain, and level accusations around the office.

You may have to stay on top of how their recommendations and solutions are presented. If the real issue is a personality conflict with another team member, you might get solutions that are somewhat less than desirable:

> "Just fire Bob. Then everything will be fine."

> Hint: It is likely that firing Bob will have little or no effect on this person's whining and complaining. He will soon find another person to be disgruntled with. This is probably how he approaches life in general.

Or if they not happy in general with much of anything,

> "Trash the project. It's an albatross."
>
> It might be, but until they specify why they feel the project should be trashed and make a detailed presentation of their reasoning, you won't know. Chances are they are trying to avoid doing any work to present their concerns intelligently (it is much easier to whine and complain in general), much less work toward solutions to them.

When you are resolute about bringing things out in the open and insisting on a solution-oriented approach, much of this type of behavior will dissipate.

Conflicts

It is very common for a good bit of complaining by one or more colleagues to be predicated by personality issues between team members. Bringing issues into the open and having people seek solutions are important tools you can use, but you also may need to work at mending some fences as a mentor.

Keep in mind that **differences** about how people approach their work and life are the most common cause of difficulty between people. You may not be able to get people to see eye-to-eye, but you can insist that people dialogue together, seek understanding, and approach their work professionally. (See next chapter on "Mediation.")

Questions and Ideas for Contemplation

Whining, complaining, blaming, and general negativity are signs of low self-worth. People don't change over night. They don't change just because we want them to or because we tell them to, "Look on the bright side," either. Helping them to feel better about their work and how they fit in at work can be a catalyst for change.

A positive, supportive environment at work sets the stage for being successful with many types of difficult situations and difficult personalities. This chapter and the previous chapter are key to "Understanding and Working with Difficult People." Keep these ideas in mind as we discuss other difficult behaviors and how best to approach them. Acknowledgment, Appreciation, and Recognition should always be part of the mix in your work with difficulties.

Sometimes you also have to be firm and insistent about what you will or will not accept within your team. By bringing things out in the open and insisting on a solution-oriented approach to concerns, you set the stage for how your team works through all problems that arise.

Try thinking through a situation you have dealt with in the past. What techniques did you use to help mitigate the concern? What skills and techniques might you apply now that you feel might make even more of a difference in dealing with the same type of concern?

Chapter 23

Mediation

When people just don't get along

It's those Differences

People are different – it is the most common cause of angst*
between people.

*upset, frustration, tension, anxiety, perturbation

Sometimes it is very hard to understand why two people can't see
eye to eye. Often it is very difficult, even impossible, to figure out
what specifically created the rift that exists between them. They
probably don't even know themselves – little frustrations grew,
egos clashed, and over time they ended up not speaking to each
other unless absolutely necessary. Now it has reached a point
where the smallest things set them off.

The truth is it probably started because they just didn't see eye-to-
eye about something.

As an example:

> A common area of contention between team members is
> the frustration that develops between a person whose
> primary focus and intent is to **get things right** and a
> colleague who really likes to **get things done**. The 'get it
> right' person may very quickly get on the 'get it done'
> person's nerves because he/she feels like they are always
> dragging their feet, while the 'get-it-right' person gets
> irate because he/she always feels pressured by his/her
> 'get it done' colleague The battle is joined, and if there is
> poor communication and little understanding the in-
> fighting and misunderstandings can get more and more
> picky.

"He said…"

"She is…"

"I can't…"

"I'm right…"

"You're wrong…"

"He did…"

Etc.

However, you can be sure that their egos are involved – and not much self-worth.

> Author's Note: As team leader, manager, coach, mentor, and educator I think I have seen it all. I certainly have experienced people who just couldn't get along under any circumstances – loathing might be too mild a term to describe their animosity toward each other. There are skills and techniques you can use to ease this type of inner-team tension and to help make things better. You will need your best listening skills, a willingness to get things out in the open, and lots of patience.

Keep in mind that it would be very unusual for a team to have no personality issues or conflicts at all. Egos are at work, and egos tend to demand satisfaction.

Understanding the Battlefield

Keep your fingers on the pulse of what is happening in your team. When you pay attention to your players, you will quickly develop a sense of how people interact, how they get along, and where the hot spots are. By staying on top of your team and how they feel, you will be able to address problems as they arise. You can also, very likely, be able to use your fundamental understanding of the personality dynamics of team members to adjust key relationships so that many problems are avoided.

For example:

> If you know that Bob and Ted are often at odds with each other over picky little details, you might wisely, if feasible, put them on different projects that keep their

interactions to a minimum. Or you might put a key mentor-type on their team when they do have to work together and give this person a heads-up that issues may arise between the two.

Don't expect to solve personality issues. Your goal is to have a team that works well together and gets along well enough that personality issues don't hamper the quality and production of your group.

When issues between team members arise, your first line of defense is to bring these issues out in the open. Don't let something fester and get out of hand.

Ego

When people aren't getting along, their egos are involved. If you ask them, they will deny up and down that they have any personal investment in the situation, but believe me, they always do. It often boils down to "I'm right, and you're wrong."

> Being RIGHT almost always has to do with ego,
>
> and very rarely has to do with really needing to be right.

You can help people move away from needing to be right by getting them to talk about their concerns and issues. It probably will not be a slam dunk, 'this will solve the problem' right away, but it will help prevent issues becoming considerably more difficult as egos fester behind the scenes.

When serving as a mentor and mediator for disputes between disgruntled employees, keep in mind that these types of concerns almost always include – the need to be right, control issues, and power issues.

Do's

Do get people talking

Your best approach is probably to meet with the antagonists separately first and then to offer a mentored dialogue if you feel it would be helpful. The better you understand the relationship and concerns, the easier it will be to help them find a meeting ground. You may need to insist that everyone be willing to discuss their concerns openly. Otherwise things that remain hidden can fester and cause future concerns.

Do listen

Listening is your best skill and technique (See Chapter 20, "Communicating in Difficult Situations."). When people feel they have had their say and feel they have been understood, then being **right** is not always so important any more. Whether you are working with someone individually or in a mediation session, help them to say what they need to say and let them know that you are listening and understanding their concerns.

Do seek solutions

Get everyone involved working toward intelligent solutions and compromises. Real issues need everyone's input. Imagined issues will likely dissipate when brought into the open and focused on with a view toward finding answers. Differences in perception can be examined more closely with an eye to everybody involved understanding different points of view. This may obviate the need for a resolution or make it easier to find a common ground for accepting one.

Do make decisions when needed

Sometimes you have to be firm and insistent. Do so kindly and with every effort to be fair. The more transparent and open you can be the better for all concerned. Avoiding difficult decisions can be extremely detrimental to your team's morale. Be sure to explain your own reasoning and the decision-making process. Even when you need to make a decision that is less than acceptable to one side or the other, they will at least see that you have considered everything carefully and will understand how and why you made the decision.

Remember to couch decisions in terms of what is best for your team and the organization. That way, though you may have to go against someone's wishes, they will know why this particular solution was chosen.

Do acknowledge, appreciate and recognize

Paying positive attention and regard to someone can help ease concerns and decisions that need to be made.

Do follow up

See how everyone involved is doing. This shows further appreciation for what they feel is important. This can be especially important when you have had to make some hard decisions that are not necessarily popular. It helps you keep up on how people are feeling and it shows them that you do care.

Don'ts

Don't take sides

This is not about who is right or wrong. It is about understanding and finding ways for people to successfully work together. On the rare occasion where there is a right and wrong, then you will need to use your leadership and mentoring skills to make a decision that everyone understands is for the best. Keep it out in the open and let them know why you are making this particular decision.

When you listen carefully to both sides and work with everyone involved giving each the opportunity to be heard, it is more likely they will understand your motives and reasoning for making a decision, particularly if that decision does lean one way or another.

Don't let things slide

You may feel you don't always have the time to work with disgruntled employees, but the truth is you can't afford not to take the time, because down the road they will take up much more of your time if things get out of hand. You also set a precedent by letting your team members know that unacceptable behaviors will not be condoned and that you will follow through with any concerns that arise.

People learn the unspoken dynamics of a workplace as well as, or better than the spoken or written ones. When you set an example for dealing with concerns, a troublemaker will probably think more than twice about making waves in your neck of the woods.

Don't let things get out of hand

If you feel a mediation session is appropriate, be sure everyone understands the purpose, the ground rules, and how you intend to approach things. Be a leader – maintain control and guide the proceedings.

Being a Mediator

If you are in a leadership position, you probably already have a great many mediation skills in your repertoire. The following are some key ideas in addition to what is above:

> Let everyone know they will have a chance to talk about their concerns, suggestions, etc. It is very important to tell them up front how and what you plan to do and who will be involved. A person who regularly uses difficult behaviors to get what they want will take every opportunity to blame and complain. You could be next on their list. When you keep things out in the open, they won't have much of a leg to stand on.

> Set parameters for how the session will proceed – you don't have to follow any particular formula, but be sure everyone understands how you intend to keep control of what transpires.

> Be kind – I firmly believe it is important to emphasize to everyone present that while people may feel upset and frustrated, a kind, professional discussion is the goal.

> Take immediate control if things even hint at getting out of hand – be a leader, be firm when you have to, insist on cordiality.

> Ask – don't forget this key skill. Asking acknowledges a person and it helps you seek understanding.

> Try to get to the root of the concern. You may not get there, and people may not even know how they got to this point of contention, but the dialogue will help open things up and let them know that you are concerned and want to help.

> Encourage solution-oriented thinking – when people focus on finding answers, they typically don't keep going back

to their frustrations and upset. Move people toward finding ways to solve their disagreements and concerns. Help them be personally proactive. Complaints and blaming should immediately trigger a move toward helping them find a means to resolve the problem at hand.

Set the stage for the future – let them know that this is only one dialogue and that you expect them to keep things out in the open and to discuss concerns that may arise either together, with you, or with another mentor in the future. When people understand that their behavior at work is important to you, they will make more of an effort to stay within acceptable parameters even though they still have issues with a fellow worker.

Questions and Ideas for Contemplation

The keys to successful mediation are:

Maintaining control

Opening up dialogue

Listening and Understanding – asking

Seeking solutions

Following-up

You may not solve personality issues between people but it is highly likely that you can resolve concerns that impact the work environment of your team.

A good exercise: what are key parameters you would set for a meeting between two disgruntled employees who have a history of interpersonal work concerns? Be flexible when possible, but try to write down key ideas that you feel would help keep the dialogue open and yet set the stage for a calm and in-control approach.

Learn as you go – your personal style and the stage you have set as a leader will help dictate your role and presence as a mediator. Use your best skills, but be sure to take mental notes about what works well and what doesn't. Build on these as you develop your mediation techniques.

Recommended: Review Chapter 9, "Keys to Boss/Employee Communications," and Chapter 20, "Communicating in Difficult Situations."

Chapter 24

Incompetent, Unmotivated, Under-achieving

Team members who have lowered affect may be reacting to personal or work concerns. Understanding who they are and what is important to them may be the key to getting them out of their lethargy. Sometimes it all comes down to what a person needs, wants, and desires.

Incompetent

True incompetence is rare. A person who is hired into a company today usually has specific credentials, education, and experience. They are theoretically at least competent at what they have been hired to do. What is more typical is that someone has moved into a job or position that is beyond their expertise and abilities. The first choice solution: get them on the right seat in the bus. (Collins)

Unmotivated

The vast majority of people want to do well and be seen in a positive light. If they seem to be unmotivated in their current job it could be due to a variety of factors. Making sure they are working at the right job, as well as making an effort to understand what their needs, wants, and desires are, may be key to helping them turn their work life around.

Underachieving

In the right seat on the bus, but not producing? Finding out what is blocking a person's ability or desire to produce may be all it takes to get them moving in the right direction.

You could Ask

The best approach to any of these concerns is to ask. Even if you are dealing with a very passive personality, they will probably be willing to open up and tell you what is important to them when you are patient and kind.

> "Mark, I noticed that your numbers have dropped significantly for the quarter. Do you want to talk about it? Can you tell me what I can do to help?"

> "Nancy, I'd like to help you get on top of your game here. Ever since you joined us you seem to be dispirited and not quite on top of things. What do you need to turn this around? What can we do to get you running up to speed?"

Getting someone who is unmotivated or underachieving talking about what would really make a difference for them at work can help get them on the bandwagon. You and fellow team members may need to continue to work with them for an extended period of time as their current approach to work may have become ingrained, but you can be successful.

Sometimes just moving someone into the right job with the right support will change their behavior patterns overnight. You can't succeed with them unless you ask and then make an effort to support them in ways that are feasible for your team and organization.

> **What do they need to do their job well?**

> **What do they want that would make them feel better about what they are doing?**

> **What are their desires as part of this particular team, about their current job, about the future?**

It IS often about understanding someone. When we make that effort, things begin to fall into place for them and how they relate to the team and team goals. As a result they also become better able to ask for what they feel they need.

Get them a Mentor

Mentorship is very much about paying attention to someone. Acknowledgment and appreciation can go a long way toward motivating someone who hasn't quite been able to get things going. Your choice does not necessarily have to be someone within your team. Sometimes the best mentors are chosen from another area or department. This helps avoid inner team conflicts and prior concerns creeping into the mix.

Important: Mentorship is not and should not be a one-shot get together. It would probably be wise to set some guidelines for your mentors to establish frequency, purpose, etc. If at all feasible, a training program would also be very helpful. If not, then you may want to have at least a brief session with them to discuss approach and goals. Make sure your mentors follow through with regular meetings and support, while making sure you keep in touch with how things are progressing.

Mentorship can be a very useful and successful tool if everyone is committed to the **process**. It offers acknowledgment, appreciation, support, and training; and under "good to great" circumstances, camaraderie, friendship, and a sense of being cared for. (Collins)

Training

Incompetence may easily be solved by getting someone up to speed and confident about what they are doing. Very few people want to do a lousy job at something. We all like the feeling of accomplishment and pride in a job well done. Understand what a person needs to get there and that may be the major part of the battle toward being successful with them.

Motivational concerns might be helped by some appropriate seminars and materials that help a person refocus their energy. These can be individually-based or team-based.

> Individual-focused materials help a person work at their own pace and give them the time and opportunity to make personal changes and to be successful.

> Team-based materials help everyone reflect on the things that matter and also have the advantage of not singling any one person out.

Use what you feel may be most successful for the specific situation and the individual concerns you are trying to solve. Try to provide training and materials that are tailored to your needs. Many individual coaches and smaller companies make this effort. It tends to be more problematic for larger training groups or corporations to have this type of flexibility.

Underachievers may find that training opens doors for them and helps them get out of the 'same-ol, same'ol' mode. You may find that they can get excited and energized about developing certain skills. Following appropriate training, they may be off and running with the ball.

Set Parameters

It wouldn't be unusual for people to be somewhat clueless about what is expected of them. In today's business environment people often get left on the sidelines while everyone else is plowing full speed ahead. That is great for self-motivators, but not so good for those who feel a bit lost. Help people understand their place on your team. Often it is important to specify duties and expectations. It may be all that is needed to help them begin to turn their work-life around.

Personal Issues

Difficulties at work may be aggravated by serious personal concerns outside of work. You can always offer support and compassion. Often there are organizational venues available that can help people deal with personal concerns. When appropriate, offer the assistance you can and help point them in the right direction. Always ask permission to offer support.

> "Carl you have been looking a bit down recently. Is there anything I can do to help?"

> "Fran, Gary told me you have been missing a good bit of work because of concerns at home. Is there anything I or the organization can do to help out? We have many support venues here at work, and I will make every effort to get the help you need."

Unmotivated and Underachieving and likely to remain so

On rare occasions you might run into an employee who is "just biding my time until retirement," or simply taking advantage of the system. In those cases you might have some hard decisions to make. If they are consistently impacting your team's ability to produce quality products and/or affecting your team's motivation, then you may want to take action.

While some managers unscrupulously might hand such an employee off to another team or division, you do have other, less disruptive, choices.

> Continue to work with them toward getting them involved in some way with your team's success.

> Move them into a position on your team or give them responsibilities that have less of an impact on your team's success.

> Gather data and evidence, especially through evaluative processes, so they can be let go – be sure to be diligent in providing cause and effect support for your decision and keeping them informed of what you are doing and why. Always offer them a means to be successful so that ultimately the decision you make is based on their failure to produce within specified goals and parameters.

Very few people really want to 'do nothing.' As a coach I have always found that people who are unmotivated and/or underachieving have a willingness to get back into gear if they feel supported and feel a part of what is happening around them. The question then becomes one of whether you and your team want to make the potentially long effort to get them to this point, or whether it makes better fiscal and time management sense to let them go.

It is your team

You set the stage and make a difference. Even if you have taken over an underachieving, unmotivated group, there is much you can do to turn things around – and quickly. Remember the whole theme of the first part of this book is about Leadership and making a difference BEFORE there are concerns. The same skills and techniques work when there ARE concerns to start with.

Make a personal commitment to make changes and then dig in. It will take time and effort and you will probably run into some roadblocks and disappointments along the way.

> Author's Note: From personal experience as a leader and as a coach of leaders, there seems to be a critical juncture within three to six months where a difficult management situation someone has been stuck with begins to turn

around. Part of that is people getting used to the new boss and the new way of doing things, but the major positive changes that take place are the direct result of the leader's commitment to excellence as exemplified in values and the qualities they espouse.

Questions and Ideas for Contemplation

This would be an excellent time to review the key concepts in the first part of this book, specifically:

Leadership

> Integrity
>
> Honesty
>
> Ownership
>
> Responsibility
>
> Caring

And "The Seven Keys to Understanding and Working with Difficult People"

> Self-Awareness
>
> Self-Worth
>
> Self-Confidence
>
> Self-Control
>
> Honesty
>
> Kindness
>
> Positivity

The two most important? Hard to say, but think hard about **Caring** and **Kindness.**

How can you use these key ideas to be successful with those employees who seem Incompetent, Unmotivated, and Underachieving?

> Hint: Help them to become aware of the importance of these concepts.

Chapter 25

Aggressive, Rude, Obnoxious

Stepping out of acceptable boundaries

Outward aggression is rarely seen in the western business arena today. When it is obvious, it is often a manager, boss, supervisor interacting with a subordinate,* however, any type of volatile or physical aggression is assumed to be verboten. The tendency is to internalize our upset and frustration in hopes of avoiding negative outcomes at work and try to deal with these in other ways. People are not always successful and the stifling of emotions can come out in many ways – perhaps the reason for this work Trilogy.**

*See Dr. Koob's, *Succeeding with Difficult Bosses* for the knowledge and tools to deal with aggressive managers and supervisors.

***Succeeding with Difficult Coworkers, Succeeding with Difficult Bosses*, and this book, *Managing Difficult Employees*

Choose safety first

Never put anyone at risk. If there is any indication that anyone could be hurt in any way you should get assistance from an appropriate department at work and report the concern immediately. Do not take chances with any potentially volatile or violent situation. Fear is a powerful motivator and there is no room for anyone having to work in an environment based on trepidation of what someone else might do.

Aggression is in the eyes of the beholder

Behavior does not have to be demonstrative to be seen as aggressive. A shy, passive employee may find a confident, forceful, pushy-type excessively obnoxious and aggressive. Just as two people who 'have words with each other' on a regular basis may see each other as being demanding and aggressive.

Perceptions ARE everything when working with people. A wise leader has enough contact with his team members to have a good feel for the dynamics that are at work between his/her players.

Self-worth

Ideally we would all like to be self-confident and in-control. It would be great if all of our employees were rooted in their personal worth and didn't need to boost their egos and need to control others through the games they often play at work for one-upmanship. The truth is egos are almost always at work in the office and though our task is not to be a psychological guru for everyone on our team, in a sense our task IS to be a psychological guru for everyone on our team – at least from the standpoint of maintaining a healthy work environment where our team is producing quality and quantity for the organization.

It is called **leadership** and it involves a proactive approach to developing a safe and enjoyable work environment as well as being a coach and mentor.

The BEST tactics...

Everything written in the first part of this book – Keys include:

>Getting out there and knowing your people – so you can respond quickly to concerns that arise

>Reinforcing the positive

>Acknowledging them and their concerns

>Appreciating them on a regular basis for their good work and positive approach to work

>Recognizing them for their efforts and success

>Catching concerns early and being willing (brave enough) to make a difference

>Caring about your people – they WILL know and it WILL make a difference

When you lead in a positive, honest, and straight-forward manner that is rooted in your own integrity, you will set an example that will help keep your team humming on an even keel. However, problems can and will occur. Be willing to deal with aggression directly, firmly, and with a good bit of kindness and compassion thrown in.

Aggression

Typically aggression in the workplace is seen as someone being pushy, bullying, and/or over-the-top. Be aware that the aggressor may not see themselves that way at all. Sometimes the simple solution to this type of behavior is to make the aggressor aware of how someone else sees them. Not always, but often, the perpetrator will make an effort to change their approach.

It is important to keep in mind that even when someone is willing to change, personal change takes time and effort. Another part of this type of success formula is to have all parties on board the change program you set in motion. They all need to be aware that an effort is being made to make personal changes, but it is possible, even likely, that old behaviors may resurface. It is also important to keep the communication doors wide open so that everyone has a forum to further pursue issues. Just this knowledge can help keep things moving in the right direction and help avoid further concerns.

Open it up

Talking with the perpetrator and the person who feels they are a victim in these circumstances is absolutely key. When you get this more out in the open, almost always the behavior will change. You might have to keep apprised of the situation for a period of time as it is not unusual for aggressive-types to use alternative tactics (e.g. passive-aggressive behaviors – see next chapter) as a means of continuing to feel in-control.

Ego, control, and power issues are often at the root of aggressive behaviors. Poor self-worth is the cause. That is why paying attention, positive attention, to your people can be extremely effective in keeping negative behaviors at a minimum.

Listen

Listen carefully to all sides of the story. Poor self-worth is motivating both sides of this coin. Let them talk it through thoroughly and you will already be on top of the situation.

Be firm and direct

If the behavior does not improve, you may need to have a heart-to-heart with the perpetrator. Keep everything above board and avoid negativity, but let them know that disruptive and controlling behaviors will not be tolerated on your team. If necessary, you can set performance guidelines that are attached to the formal evaluative process (See Appendix I for ideas related to formal evaluations). Don't let this type of behavior slide as it can escalate quickly if the situation is exacerbated in any way.

'Picking-on' behavior

There are negative, aggressive (and passive-aggressive) personalities that have such a low self-worth that they seem to need someone to put down or feel 'better than' to feel comfortable with themselves. It is common for this type of person to shift their 'picking-on' behavior to another person when their actions have been thwarted with their current victim. Make sure they understand that the behavior is unacceptable under any and all circumstances on your team.

Rudeness

Again, it often is about perceptions. I may not see a person's behavior as rude, but my shy administrative assistant might. Bringing the behavior, very specifically, to the attention of the perpetrator is often enough to have them make an effort to change. Discussions with both parties, and often a mediation together, can be very successful if done as openly, controlled, positively, and kindly as is feasible.

Obnoxious

Unacceptable behaviors are often predicated by differences between people. I may not like how you do something, or how you say things and vice-versa. Openness, and a willingness to listen to all sides of an equation that lead to understanding, are your best tools. Ingrained angst caused by differences between people may be harder to solve and take a bit more effort and time, but the tactics are the same. Get the people involved talking about their concerns and their own perspective. Understanding may not make things perfect and acceptable, but can help ease much of the angst between antagonists.

Again simple awareness of how things are being perceived change the dynamics of the interrelationships. That awareness will often lead to efforts to change how someone approaches another and how someone's approach is being interpreted.

Follow-up

It is very important to keep in touch with how this type of mediation progresses. When the key players understand that you will be available when necessary, more effort will likely be made to continue to improve the situation. Don't keep a vigil or make people nervous by hovering; just keep your finger on the pulse of how things are going. Those walks about the office or lab will keep you on top of much that happens with your team members. [See Chapter 6, "Walk, Listen, Learn, Follow-Up"]

Self-worth

Difficult behaviors are rooted in poor self-worth. Whenever possible work from the ground up; hence the emphasis in the first part of this book on building your own awareness and clear leadership. Set the stage and you will have far fewer difficulties to deal with and when they do arise you will have a solid foundation of integrity and trust to work from. It will make all the difference in the world.

Remember – your own self-worth and self-confidence are major keys to your success.

Questions and Ideas for Contemplation

DO work from a positive, kind, compassionate and understanding approach as often as possible. There are ALWAYS ways to deal with people kindly.

DON'T ignore or try to solve potentially volatile or violent situations yourself. Get help. While you may be able to work through a difficult situation, backup is always wise and you can never be sure when you may need the help.

Take some time to think through some scenarios with the types of aggressive behaviors discussed above. What tactics would you take? How would you approach everyone involved? What would be your key strategies? How would you make sure you stayed on top of this concern in the future?

Write out some key ideas. This can help serve as an initial plan if a problem does arise on your team.

Chapter 26

Passive-Aggressive
Surreptitious Behaviors

Often it is the behind-the-scenes maneuvers for control and power that can have the most devastating impact on a team's morale. A person who uses passive-aggressive behaviors typically works with people in less obvious ways to get what he/she wants. Passive-aggressive behaviors can include:

Innuendo

Spreading rumors

Behind-the-back tactics

Lying

Cheating

Taking credit for another's work or taking someone's work

Back-stabbing

Get it out in the OPEN!

Surreptitious behavior doesn't stand a chance if people become aware of what is happening. The perpetrators of this type of behavior will quickly understand that you have no intention of letting their behind-the-back tactics continue if you call them on it. The question that remains then is how to bring these under-handed, behind-the-back behaviors out in the open.

Have you ever received complaints like these?

> "Joe, you need to know that David is always spreading rumors about me around the office. It is really upsetting me and I can't work here anymore unless you get him off my back."

"Ernestine is always stealing my ideas when I leave my desk. Can I get an office with a lock on the door?"

"I want you to know that I did most of the work on the Johnson contract and Frank's out their bragging it was all his. I'm tired of playing second fiddle to that guy."

Or a thousand others similar to these?

The only thing you know from these statements is that there is some type of bad blood between the antagonists. Your job, and it isn't always easy or pleasant, is to find out the truth – "Just the facts, ma'am" (Joe Friday)

Getting to the bottom

It takes tact and kindness to find out what is really going on in many of these types of situations.

> There may be a good bit of truth in what this person is relating to you.

> Or the opposite may be closer to the truth – there may be a long-held rivalry and this person is trying to get you to buy into their side of things.

> Or, what is most common, is that the answer lies somewhere in the middle.

Open things up by using your best two skills: asking and listening

> "Mitch, what I hear you telling me is that David is saying things around the office that you feel are damaging to you personally. I am willing to look into this, but you will need to provide me with more details about specific incidents. We will need to sit down and go through this carefully. You also need to understand that I will need to talk with others in the office, including David to fully understand what is happening."

You are letting Mitch know:

> That you are concerned about his claim and that you take him seriously

> That you are willing to follow-up

> That he needs to supply you with additional information

178

and that you will listen carefully

That you are not just going to take his word, but want to get to the truth

That other people will know about this concern as well

That ultimately you will hear David's side of the story, too.

In other words you are setting the stage and parameters for the resolution of the concern.

If Mitch doesn't completely back away from the complaint at this point, you can set the ball rolling. Even if he does back away, it might be wise to dig a little deeper with him about this issue so he gets a clear message that you are not going to let whining and complaining about fellow team members slide by.

One of the key ideas here is that when you take this type of approach, and do so several times with your team, they will get to know that you WILL deal with concerns openly and honestly and that you have specific strategies (which they will pick up on quickly) as to how you go about working through this type of scenario.

Keep in mind that people who typically use behind-the-back tactics as a means to get what they want will try other ways to gain the upper hand. That is why following up with everyone involved will help keep things above board.

Proceed with kindness

Set the stage further by making time for you and Mitch to sit down and talk through the complaint. Use your best asking and listening skills and make sure you get Mitch to delineate his complaint as thoroughly as possible. Get specific examples and make sure that Mitch has a chance to talk about any concerns he may have with David (and others).

If appropriate, you may want to ask several other trusted team members, who might have knowledge of this dyad, about the complaint, how they perceive this relationship, and what their understanding is. Keep things out in the open without pointing fingers. Make sure they understand that you are seeking the truth and want to alleviate concerns.

When dealing with this type of issue between team members, you have to make a command decision about whether it is appropriate to talk about specific people or not. Confidentiality can be both good and detrimental depending on how you weigh many factors. Use your best judgment and be sure to let everyone know what you are doing, and why, if you feel it is important to bring out specifics.

Set up a time with David to get his side of the story. You don't necessarily have to, and some times it is wise not to, specify who has made the complaint, at least not initially. Here is a possible approach.

"David, I have heard some concerns about your making inappropriate and inaccurate statements about another team member around the office. It is important for me to hear your side of the story. For now I would like to keep things confidential while I try to understand what is happening. My intent is not to blame anyone, but to understand how we can resolve this concern for everyone in the best and least disruptive way possible. How would you respond to this?"

You might get anything from, "I don't know what you are talking about," to an explosion like, "That jerk Mitch has been blaming me for stuff again hasn't he." Be prepared; you might get an earful.

You need to remain calm, in-control, and continue to try to understand the root of the problem. You may have to be persistent in the face of resistance. These are often not easy discussions to have as the feelings on both sides can run deep. You might find that the basis is a long underlying feud between two team members that is rooted in bad feelings and ego games. Then you will need to apply your leadership and mediation skills to help resolve the conflict (see Chapter 23).

Author's Note: Even though this may take some effort and very careful handling, it is better to get it out in the open than to let it continue to fester. From long experience dealing with these types of concerns and the mediations between feuding employees, I have found that these difficult relationships at work will erupt again and again unless you are willing to work through them.

Get them on board a solution

An important part of the follow-up to listening and understanding is getting all parties involved in a proactive, solution-oriented approach to the concern. When they are involved, they feel they have some control, and that can help things have a positive foundation for your team members toward dealing with these issues now and in the future.

Your goal is to help them to understand that your team is not the arena for internal feuds and underhanded behaviors. These two antagonists may never like each other or become buddies, but you can succeed in having them understand that disruptive behaviors will be dealt with; and you can work with them toward an understanding that they can work together in spite of their differences with each other.

The Key Idea

Regardless of people's reactions, and the subsequent work you have to do to ameliorate the situation, you have succeeded in several ways:

> You have brought it out in the open, so the behavior is no longer behind-the-back
>
> People know you will not put up with negative, surreptitious behavior
>
> They also know that you will seek understanding, the truth, and a resolution

Who is to Blame?

There is almost always some finger-pointing in these types of situations – typically in both directions. You should not take sides. Even if someone is at fault, there is usually considerably more behind-the-scenes than the initial complaint. Get to the root and avoid blame whenever possible.

If you have a person in the office who seems to be a regular perpetrator of behind-the-scenes innuendo and turmoil, they will still get the message loudly and clearly that you will not put up with this type of behavior.

When an individual does seem to be the primary troublemaker, there are still usually two (or more) apples in the pie. It is very helpful for everyone involved to understand how they may be adding to the mix, even if indirectly, by their own behaviors. By getting everyone involved in resolving the dispute, you can avoid most finger-pointing on your part. By maintaining a calm, in-control and non-judgmental approach you set an example for everyone.

Keep in mind that by acting on this you speak volumes about how you expect people to treat each other. It is important to keep your key values and qualities at the forefront when working with these types of difficult situations.

Complaining

Revisiting this here is probably appropriate:

> Complaints, if taken verbatim, cause sides to be taken and battle lines drawn. Always find out what is behind the concern – what the dynamics of the situation and relationship are.

> Listen and ask

> Mediate

Most importantly get the complainer on board helping to find a solution. Inveterate complainers typically don't want to have anything to do with solving their concern. They just want to get others to buy into their negativity, or to get others in trouble. Castigating others helps them to feel superior; it is one way they draw attention to themselves.

By putting the onus on their own shoulders to find solutions you make complaining a difficult behavior to continue. In other words, when it doesn't get them what they want, the complaining behavior wanes.

Questions and Ideas for Contemplation

Surreptitious behaviors can be the hardest and most time consuming to handle. However, if you are willing to open these concerns up and get them out in the open, after a few efforts the perpetrator(s) will get the idea that he/she needs to change their ways because it isn't worth all the fuss. You may not change the person, but you can curb the behavior.

Building self-worth

As in all difficult behaviors, behind-the-back behaviors are rooted in negative self-worth. Help the perpetrator develop a more solid sense of self and you will solve the problem at the root. Motivational training, assertiveness workshops, coaching, etc., may be wise investments when dealing with a difficult personality. It may be worth looking into. Again, you may not change the person a great deal, but you will open their eyes a good bit in the process and they will very likely change the behavior while on your team because the behavior is no longer getting them what they want.

Chapter 27

Passive Behavior

"I can't get anything out of her. It's like she's afraid to say anything."

"Gary just won't make any decisions. I'm gung ho to get something off the ground and I run into this brick wall."

"He's so quiet; I never know what's going on."

Passive people rarely cause trouble directly. The difficulty typically comes when a more outgoing and aggressive person works with them. These types of frustrations can escalate fairly quickly if two people with very different approaches to the world collide on a team.

Passivity

A passive person may be shy and it will take considerable positive contact for them to feel comfortable enough to interact easily with others.

They may simply be quiet, i.e. "a man (or woman) of few words."

They may feel threatened by others who are more outgoing, boisterous, and energetic.

They may be more deliberate about how they go about things and demand of themselves exceptionally high quality above all else.

Support and Encourage

The best approach with passive personalities is to get everyone on board a positive, supportive approach to bringing them out of their reluctance to engage. Efforts to acknowledge and appreciate them will help a great deal, but one of the real keys is regular – daily, if feasible – friendly contact:

"Hi Jan, just thought I'd stop by and see how you were doing. Any questions about anything? I'm glad you're on board."

E-mail: "Hey, Steve, just thought I'd touch base today. Anything I can do to help?"

"John, how is it going? You are looking good. Keep up the hard work!"

"Sally, I appreciated your getting back to me on the Stevens contract. Thanks. Keep it coming."

"Nice tie, Ted. I like your sense of style."

These types of interactions may seem time-consuming and unnecessary, especially considering your busy schedule, but they can mean a lot to a person who feels out of place or ignored. Simple, basic, kind communications don't take much time and they can mean much more than anyone may think to a person who has felt/feels out of sync at work and/or at odds with the world in general.

Don't expect a reaction or response. Patience is very important. Over time they will typically start to open up. Progress may be slow and any negativity and particularly any frustration will shut down all the good work you and team members may have accomplished to that point.

Don't expect them to change their personality. Your goal is to help them be more interactive within the scope of your team and what you are trying to accomplish. Helping other team members understand that the dynamics in working with this type of personality will probably always be different from what they expect helps them to deal with some of the frustrations they may feel. When they understand that encouragement, support, and patience will make a difference, they will be more likely to use those techniques to help their colleague succeed.

Reinforce positive behavior patterns

Be sure to encourage the more outgoing behaviors that they exhibit. Again, progress may be slow, but if you reinforce what you want to see, they will often open up even more.

"Karl, I'm glad you spoke up at the meeting today. What

you had to say was important and I appreciate the succinct way that you brought it forward. It was easy to understand and created some lively discussion. Good job!"

"Beth, that was a great report you turned in. You should feel good about what you have accomplished and I am happy that you and Pete were able to work on this together. Keep up the good work."

Most people want to be engaged, but it is not necessarily easy for them. Kindness, encouragement, and support can help a lot over time. Keep the compliments flowing.

When you do have to get things moving

Sometimes you and your team need to move things along in the production process. Keep the support and encouragement part of your approach:

"Lyle, I know you don't like to be pushed, but I'm going to need your data by Thursday at three. This is a firm deadline for me, so your work is critical. Let me know if you need any support in getting this done on time. Thanks. I really appreciate the job you are doing."

Get in plenty of positivity and kudos, but be sure to set parameters. Structure can be very helpful in keeping people on track. Be sure that when you do set parameters and specific guidelines that everyone follows them and that you don't let things slide. (See Chapter 7, "Bureaucracy and Chapter 8, Time Management" for a discussion of this important concept.)

Be sure to follow up with thanks and kudos for work well done.

If problems and missed deadlines occur, then it is important to let people know as kindly as possible that this concern is affecting team performance.

"Lyle, I need to know what you need from me and the other project members to help you keep important deadlines. Part of what makes this team successful is the ability of each of us to interact, support, and encourage each other. Let's take some time to talk this through…"

There are always more positive ways to follow through with concerns. A kind, gentle approach works best for everyone.

Questions and Ideas for Contemplation

Passivity can be very frustrating to other members of your team as well as to you. A proactive campaign to help draw a passive personality more into the mainstream of the office dynamics is the best approach. However, when problems do occur, it is your job as a leader to keep things rolling and to heal wounds and divisions that may occur. Use your best leadership skills and find the most supportive ways to approach concerns.

If you have a shy or unresponsive person on your team, brainstorm ways in which you and your team members can support and encourage their blossoming and becoming more involved dynamically in the office. It is possible to overdo this, but because of busy schedules we tend let this type of support slide. Keep in mind that frustrations can build fairly quickly when people are stressed and under the gun to produce. Find the best ways to keep your team humming along.

Chapter 28

Ambitious, Obsequious

Some employees may be frustrating to you because of their need to hype themselves and their accomplishments. As if you didn't already have enough on your plate, a fawning, effusive team member can, and will if you let them, take up a lot of your precious time.

Ambitious

Team members who are ambitious can be creative, hard-working, and productive; they can also be more hot air than substance. Use an employee's ambition to get them to focus on quality, production, and responsibility. You will know their mettle when you offer them the chance to prove themselves.

Obsequious, Flattering

While it is nice to have kudos and appreciation land in your lap on a regular basis, you have to draw some lines in the sand so that people know what you expect and understand that their success depends on living up to those criteria. The overly-fawning person can raise resentment in other team players if they feel someone is being held to different standards. Keep the playing field level.

How to

The best way to deal with ambitious and obsequious personnel is to:

Allow them to prove themselves – give them responsibility and see how they handle it; your true warriors will excel, and you will have gained a positive ally in dealing with your own time management concerns

Let them know what you value – in other words what WILL make a difference on evaluations and promotions. If everyone knows the parameters that make a difference, there can be no doubt when it comes to what success means on your team.

Set the Stage for Everyone

In Chapter 3, "Leadership," I challenged you to delineate the top values and qualities you aspired to as a leader. Revisiting this list and considering this in reference to the top values and qualities you expect your team members to exhibit is another great exercise. You may find that these values are consistent, or you may find there are other values that you feel are as, or more, important for your developing players.

You have to let them know. Be willing to spread the word regularly and through as many forums as you can:

At meetings

"I want to thank everyone who got their data to me before the three o'clock deadline yesterday. It made my job considerably easier in bringing all this together."

The message you are sending is that you value **timeliness**. You are reinforcing those who were on their game and you are sending another message to those who weren't without being overtly negative or reprimanding.

Through e-mails:

"Thanks to Tom and Judy for their exemplary work on the BeTec contract. Excellent quality and we are done two days ahead of schedule. Kudos to all who helped them along the way."

Lots of appreciation and acknowledgment here and you reinforce **quality** and **timeliness**.

In passing:

"Penny, I'm glad I ran into you. I wanted to thank you for taking responsibility for bringing the team's agenda forward at the board meeting. You did a great job. Keep up the good work."

You are acknowledging the importance of stepping up to the plate for the team through **personal responsibility**.

On the phone:

> "Oscar, thanks for being so open about the concerns we have with the current development program. I feel you opened all our eyes a bit wider on important issues. We do need to address some of these issues right away, so keep me posted on progress."

> You are reinforcing **openness** and **honesty** and the importance of tackling hard issues as well.

Speeches and other formal venues:

> "This team has produced great ideas this year and we have been successful on several fronts by running with some of these. Thanks to all for your hard work brainstorming in your development seminars and throughout the year. Kudos!"

> Giving people the heads up that **creativity** and **out-of-the-box thinking** are valued and recognized.

This is another one of those skills and techniques that can easily be incorporated into your schedule without any additional time. Unfortunately, it is also easily forgotten and we tend to let it slide. People need to hear what you value through your actions AND words. They need to hear it repeatedly and often.

The great thing about doing this on a regular basis is that it sets guidelines for all your personnel as to what IS important on your team and you can easily use these same criteria as part of the evaluative process. It is the best approach I know to dealing with those who think they can get around the system through flattery only.

Plus, when a person does try to bend your ear a bit too much, you can always refer to the many things you have kept out on the table.

> "Carl, I'm glad you appreciate the work I do. On another note, I just wanted to follow-up with you on the Stensen contract. Remember I expect it to be on my desk by four tomorrow. Keep up the good work."

Questions and Ideas for Contemplation

Take some time to delineate key values and qualities you want to encourage in your team players. Then set aside the next week to see if you can work in as many reinforcing statements as possible without adding to your busy schedule. Try to get in the habit of talking the talk.

Do you have an ambitious overly-fawning type? Follow-up their aggrandizing with a statement of purpose like the one above. They will start to get the message that substance is much more important than fluff.

Chapter 29

Prejudice, Discrimination, Bias, Sexual Harassment

Many specific concerns will cross your desk as a manager and leader. The skills and tools discussed throughout this book can serve you well. At the end of this chapter I will attach parts of the texts from Chapters 28 of my book *Succeeding with Difficult Coworkers* and 29 of my book *Succeeding with Difficult Bosses*. These discussions will give you a different slant to what is discussed immediately below. Ultimately you need to follow organization guidelines, Human Resources and legal recommendations, and your own best judgment in dealing with these types of serious issues.

Know Processes and Procedures

Your business/organization should have specific guidelines for dealing with serious issues. Make sure you know these and review these carefully before taking any steps to deal with problems of this nature. Unless, of course, it is an emergency situation and you need to make a snap decision.

Don't Hesitate

The best advice I can offer is to get on top of these types of concerns immediately. Hesitation and an attempt to put this on a back burner WILL come back to bite you. Get the involved team members into your office, understand what the concerns are, and what the dynamics of their interactions are.

Document, Document, Document

Anything and everything that is concerned with this type of situation should be documented. Get it down on paper/computer and place a file in a safe place. This includes notes on meetings (transcripts if feasible), any discussions (including those made in passing or chance meetings), all e-mails and other written communication, and all complaints and counter complaints, etc. Be sure to get down who, what, when, where, how, how much, and so on. These situations call for meticulousness in keeping materials that may prove important down the road.

Whenever possible include supportive and witness materials from other sources. It is often wise to insist that those involved put things down on paper, so that there are hard copies of the complaints, concerns, and processes.

Keep people informed

Serious issues should be addressed to appropriate people up the chain of command. You should let your superior know immediately if you are dealing with a prejudicial or harassment concern and depending on appropriate organizational processes, you will also probably want to contact Human Resources, support services, and possibly your legal department.

Bias

We are all biased about some things:

> I may not like smoking and avoid smokers like the plague

> I may prefer to work alone and get frustrated when I have to work in close proximity to someone else.

> I may not eat citrus fruit

> I may not like the color purple

> I may not like lint

Biases can be based on serious issues; or they may just be silly, or it may just seem so to us. Biases can also get out of hand, particularly with people who have a difficult history with each other. Small biases can raise the stakes in a conflict so that to the antagonists they don't seem so little anymore.

Generally speaking many issues raised in the workplace between people can be dealt with directly through discussion, understanding, openness, and kindness. If you have set your leadership stage toward having an open, caring approach to people and concerns, these situations should be relatively easy to deal with. Get the protagonists together and get them talking. Compromise is usually possible. Use your people and leadership skills to get things out in the open and get people working toward a reasonable resolution.

The key idea in dealing with biases is that if it is troubling someone enough to be concerned about the situation or becomes a problem at work, it probably needs to be dealt with in some way.

Prejudice and Discrimination

We could think of prejudice as taking biases to the next level. Prejudice is singling out a characteristic or trait and using that as the basis for treating or dealing with someone differently. Webster states:

> ...a judgment or opinion held in disregard of facts that contradict it; unreasonable bias...the holding of such judgments or opinions...suspicion, intolerance, or irrational hatred of other races, creeds, regions, occupations, etc.

One of the difficulties in dealing with prejudice is that the degree of the bias may be very difficult to delineate and to prove. The clear caveat to this is that IF a team member is concerned enough to bring an issue into your purview, or you get wind of such a concern, you should make an effort to find out what is behind it.

Common prejudices that you may have to understand and deal with as a manager/leader:

> Racial prejudice – treating someone differently because of their race
>
> Gender issues
>
> Religious
>
> Sexual preference
>
> Smoking
>
> Weight

This certainly is not an exhaustive list, but it does give you an idea of the types of concerns you may have to be concerned with. In my time as a manager I have had to work through more than a couple of these with team members.

We often refer to the types of issues above as discriminatory. When concerns arise, people feel they have been discriminated against because of some prejudice on another person's or an institution's part related to race, creed, gender, etc. These issues are often best dealt with through appropriate agencies at work. Find out what the appropriate procedures and processes are and be sure to document all complaints, actions, etc. Your leadership through these difficult issues speaks volumes to your team members about what is and is not acceptable.

Sexual Harassment/Harassment

Again, if the matter is such that someone is concerned enough to bring it up to you or others, or you witness something of concern, you need to act.

If the behavior is inappropriate to someone, it needs to be addressed.

Support

Dealing with these types of very serious issues is draining for everyone. A wise leader will make sure that the people involved receive the support they need throughout the process of resolving the issue. Be sure to take care of yourself as well.

Actions you can take

Your leadership, listening, support, and mediation skills will likely be tested to their limits when dealing with these types of issues. If you are on top of the procedural and legal ramifications of how this should be handled, then I believe there is much that you can do in-house.

> Author's Note: I have had to work through some very sticky prejudicial and harassment issues as a leader. After apprising the powers that be of these concerns, I was able to deal with them within my department. The key to this success was bringing concerned individuals in for open discussions, having mediation sessions, and working with everyone involved toward a successful resolution.
>
> I found that perpetrators and victims were both immediately amenable to dealing with these concerns

directly. Typically the perpetrator was willing to apologize for any perceived or actual concerns and to make an immediate effort to change their behavior.

In today's business environment, prejudices and harassment issues are taken very seriously. Most employees understand this and when confronted with their unacceptable behavior will back down and away from any further detrimental actions.

Follow-up

If you do handle these types of concerns within your team or department, be sure to follow-up with all the people involved. This gives everyone a heads up that you will be vigilant about these types of issues and that you will not tolerate any further inappropriate actions.

Support and positive encouragement for both victims and perpetrators from you and other team members can also help avoid future concerns.

Questions and Ideas for Contemplation

The best exercise you could do to prepare for these types of exigencies would be to develop a plan to deal with specific types of issues – a plan that is rooted in knowledge of organizational procedures and processes, and in your own personal approach. See below for some additional specific recommendations, however, thinking this through carefully will help you manage concerns that arise quickly and efficiently.

Addendum to Chapter 30

Harassing Behavior and other Legal Issues

Taken from *Succeeding with Difficult Coworkers,* and *Succeeding with Difficult Bosses* Koob

You should never tolerate behaviors that are inappropriate. Harassment can come in a variety of forms. If you are uncomfortable with behavior that seems inappropriate, discriminatory, harassing, or prejudiced there are steps you can take. We will examine a series of 'steps' that work well with approaching these types of concerns.

> Note: many companies address these issues in their employee handbooks. Use these types of documents as a reference point for further understanding and action. Regulations may dictate how you should respond to inappropriate behavior/actions. It is important to read these documents thoroughly and to take appropriate action. Fundamentally how you approach these concerns will be your decision.

Sexual Harassment

Essentially the legal description for sexually inappropriate behavior is whether a *reasonable* woman or man would find the behavior to be sexual harassment. Obviously this leaves some questions about exactly how this might be interpreted by our legal system.

However, what is most important is how the behavior affects you. If YOU feel that a behavior is inappropriate or offensive, it is probably worth taking initial steps to curtail it or deal with it by bringing your concerns forward to the person(s) perpetrating the behavior, an agency at work, and/or another authority figure. [See Note above about company regulations.]

Discrimination

Discrimination is treating someone differently because of some characteristic or trait.

For example:

> Race or ethnicity
>
> Creed or religion
>
> On the basis of gender
>
> Handicapped individuals

Specific laws cover these issues and appropriate authorities, human resources departments, and government sources can provide current information. NOTE: If at some point you feel the need to pursue your concern legally, please contact an appropriate agency and/or get a lawyer qualified in this area.

Prejudicial/Biased behavior

Prejudices can be very concerning but unfortunately they are often legally, ethically, and practically very hard to define/pin down. Well-documented concerns, however, can and should be addressed if they are causing significant problems and discomfort at work. It is not unusual for people to have minor (and even major) prejudices of which they are unaware. Drawing attention to your concern with the perpetrator (and an authority figure) may be all that is necessary for the behavior to cease.

Know your Organization's policies

If you have concerns about any type of inappropriate behavior, you should read through the policies published by your business very carefully. If you do not know where to find them, check with Human Resources. It is very important to know how these issues are expected to be handled and what options you have when you feel that your concerns have reached a point where you want and/or need support and assistance. If you have any doubts as to the proper procedures, the meaning of a guideline or policy, or what you should do next, contact a Human Resources professional and sit down and discuss your options.

Dealing with inappropriate, harassing, discriminatory, and prejudicial behaviors

If it is inappropriate to you, it is inappropriate.

Putting up with these types of behaviors, particularly over the long haul, can be very demeaning and devastating. You have the right and <u>should</u> make an effort to do something to alleviate the concern. Please note: you always have the choice of getting professional support from within your business (Human Resources or other appropriate venue) as well as legal advice, if you feel you need further guidance.

There are many issues that should be considered about what should be done when someone is approaching another person in an inappropriate and/or sexual manner.

> Legal issues abound – on both sides of the coin
>
> It can be very difficult to prove
>
> People are going to go through a tremendous amount of angst and pain
>
> It never seems like there can be a win - win situation

General considerations that can help

> First: if you feel someone is approaching you inappropriately, let them know how you feel.
>
> Do this as soon as you feel uncomfortable with what is going on. The sooner you let them know you are not happy with this type of attention the better.
>
> Do it in as kind and understanding a way as possible even if they are being obnoxious and crude.

Be firm and assertive. Don't back down. Let them know that you won't tolerate this type of behavior.

> "Kelly, I need to let you know that I am very uncomfortable with the statements you have been making toward me. I feel they are very inappropriate. I would appreciate it if you would stop."

Regardless of what they say – denial, laugh-it-off, etc., stick to your guns.

> "Kelly, I am very serious about this. I don't want to have to report this, but I will if it continues."

IMPORTANT: Document every incident and every interaction; be specific and comprehensive. If anyone witnesses the behavior, try to get them to sign your notes or make a statement that you can file, too.

Second: if the behavior does not stop, make one more attempt to reason with them. This will give you at least two specific incidents where you have documented your response to their inappropriateness and your request for them to terminate it.

> "Kelly, I asked you to please stop this sexual innuendo and what I feel are inappropriate and crude actions. If you continue I will take this immediately to the authorities. I have documented and dated everything you have said and done and my requests for you to stop."

Third: If the behavior has escalated, or if it continues after several attempts to curtail it, go to your a superior and tell him/her. Be sure you let them know that you have documentation of the inappropriate behaviors of your colleague and your responses. Also make sure they understand that you are documenting this meeting with them.

It is probably a good idea to keep this information far from prying eyes – under lock and key, encrypted, or protected by a password.

You may also want to have a copy of this material with a very close and trusted friend who is not a colleague.

Finally: If the behavior has not stopped and your boss does not seem willing to pursue this issue, take it to other appropriate resources.

Carefully Document the issues and concerns you have

Even if the documentation is only your word against theirs, the fact that you have gone to the trouble to keep detailed records gives your complaint more legitimacy. Be honest and professional regardless of the other person's behavior/approach to you.

Keep detailed notes of every instance

> The specific behavior, verbiage, actions, facial expressions, gestures, and tone of voice
>
> Date and sign each entry
>
> Keep an extra copy in a safe place – a safety deposit box is ideal. DO NOT allow access to this information to anyone unless you absolutely trust them. It is probably NOT a good idea to have this type of information stored on an office computer.
>
> Share this information with a trusted relative or friend.

Discussing your concerns with a trusted person helps you document the whole process and can provide you tremendous support. DO NOT keep these types of concerns to yourself. It is very important to let someone else know what you are concerned about and why. Be willing to be open and specific, even if the whole situation is embarrassing and awkward at first.

If anyone has been witness to any of these incidents, ask them if they would be willing to witness your account. Whether they do or not, note their presence.

You can note/document their response to your request. They may offer valuable information. Always be as specific as possible in taking notes:

> When I asked Barbara to witness Mike's sexual innuendos, she got very pale and frightened: "I really want to help you out, Ann, but I'm scared of Mike. He has threatened to fire me when I asked him to stop. Just be quiet and put up with it. He has done a lot worse. Keep quiet and be careful about this because he thinks he owns everyone in this office." She seemed genuinely scared and has avoided talking with me since this incident.

If there is another person at work who shares these same concerns, talk to them about what you are doing and ask them if they would like to keep their own records and/or work with you on resolving this joint issue. You can document your conversation with them whether they are willing to help back you up or not.

Bring it out in the open

At some point after you have taken the time to document several incidents you should bring your concerns to the attention either of someone at work or directly to the perpetrator.

> IMPORTANT: I have found that the following steps, taken in order, work extremely well. This is a personal decision and you must decide whether to take this issue to an appropriate agency at your place of work, hire legal assistance, request mediation, etc. Make sure you are comfortable with the decision you make to go forward. Only you can make this decision. Err on the side of caution and get assistance if you have any doubts. Requesting mediation is an excellent choice at this juncture.

> Only you know how serious this issue is. Please be sure to take care of yourself and to play it safe whatever your decision is to move ahead with this concern.

At your initial meeting

> Set this up as a formal, sit-down, secure meeting. Close the door when you arrive. You want this to be professional and you want your boss (colleague) to take what you have to say seriously.

> Try to be/stay calm and professional

> Try to use non-accusatory language – own what you say:

>> "John, I am concerned about one issue between us that I would like to bring up. I know you may not mean this in any negative way, but I feel very uncomfortable when you address me as "Honey," "Sweetie," "Babe," and so on. I also feel you have made some suggestive comments when we have been alone and this also makes me very uncomfortable. Could we talk about this and come to some agreement as to what we both feel is appropriate?"

> Your boss (colleague) may not have a clue that what he is doing is making you uncomfortable. And unless he has

been living with his head in the sand for the past twenty plus years, he will get the point immediately. He will very likely be embarrassed, apologize immediately, and promise to watch what he says in the future.

Document any meetings that take place relative to this issue.

Take the next step, a second meeting or take this to Human Resources or another appropriate agency at work, if the behavior does not improve or if there are further concerns. Be sure to continue your documentation.

Second meeting

NOTE: Consideration for a second meeting is an entirely personal decision. Many people feel that one meeting/warning is enough and if the behavior doesn't change, you should immediately get professional assistance in pursuing the matter further. Other people are more comfortable with making a further effort to resolve the issue themselves. This is YOUR decision and only you can determine what step(s) to take next.

If at any time you feel threatened by your boss/colleague, or your boss/colleague retaliates in some way for bringing this subject up, you should take immediate action with an appropriate department/ authority at your place of business. You may also want to consider legal advice if this happens.

In today's business environment it would be rare for a boss/ colleague not to make an effort to change an inappropriate behavior if you approached him/her in the manner described above. Most people are fully aware of the consequences of being accused of harassing or discriminatory behavior. However, if another meeting is called for because the behavior has not changed, then you need to take it to the next level.

Let him know how you feel again, but don't mince words. He needs to understand that this is a serious concern.

"John, last month I came in and discussed with you what I considered to be a very serious personal issue. I do not feel that your behavior has changed and I am very concerned. I feel that if we can't agree on how to resolve this issue I will have to take this to the next level."

Let him know that you have been continuing to document your concerns.

> "John, since the last time we met about this personal issue, I have noted and documented several additional occasions when I felt your approach to me was demeaning and had sexual overtones."

Then be willing to detail these incidences, complete with dates, times, verbiage, etc.

Strongly indicate your intention to follow through if the behavior doesn't improve immediately

> "I don't want to take this any further, but if I feel I must, I will contact Human Resources immediately if I am still uncomfortable with what is happening.

If you are very concerned at this point, it may be appropriate to have a trusted person attend this second meeting with you, or possibly include a legal representative.

Follow-through

If your boss/colleague still doesn't seem to get the message, then you need to follow through IMMEDIATELY and contact an appropriate agency and/or authority at your place of work. You may very well want to get some legal advice at this stage. A good lawyer, qualified in this area, can help you make the right decisions to take appropriate actions.

Be aware that an individual may back off for a day or two, or a week or two and then go right back to their highly inappropriate behavior pattern. Again, at this point, you should immediately follow through by reporting this behavior to an appropriate authority and department (Human Resources).

Important

As a manager and coach I have handled a number of these types of complaints in my work and I have never seen a client have to take these issues past the stage of initial contact with the perpetrator. When handled in this way, the person got the message loud and clear and the behavior stopped immediately. Sincere apologies, coupled with extreme embarrassment, were part of these resolutions. [On a number of occasions my clients requested my presence at a meeting with their perpetrator and I served as a mediator.]

Yes, you do have the legal right to pursue these types of concerns, but be aware that these can be very difficult and stressful for everyone concerned. If your boss/colleague responds appropriately and makes an effort to change his/her behavior toward you (and others), move ahead with your life and work and be thankful that there are laws and sensibilities today that keep these types of concerns from escalating.

Very important

Your safety and well-being, as well as the safety and well-being of all those who work with you, is of paramount importance. When in doubt, take the actions that are best for you and others.

Repercussions because of even an initial attempt to deal with this type of situation are possible from an egotistical, uncaring, unethical boss (colleague). Maintain your vigilance and document any concerns that may arise as a result. Though these would likely be rare if you keep things as open and professional as possible, there really are some jerks in the workplace!

Take care of yourself

Take care of yourself during any time you are dealing with unethical, inappropriate behavior. It can be a very stressful time. Support and understanding from friends and relatives is particularly helpful. I believe that sharing your concerns with a trusted relative or friend is essential throughout this whole process. This is a very heavy burden to carry alone. A professional personal coach can also provide you with valuable assistance in supporting you through this process, and also be a reliable witness if you need one.

This can be very difficult, even devastating. Do everything you can to support yourself and to have people you can turn to. You shouldn't feel guilty or blame yourself for this, though you may. You are a child of the universe and deserve to be treated kindly and honorably. Support from a qualified professional may also be very helpful in working through these types of concerns: counselor, personal coach, minister, etc.

Chapter 30

Really Difficult Behaviors

At some time in your career you will probably have someone on your team who exhibits consistent and pervasive difficult behaviors. I encourage you to use the knowledge, skills and tools discussed in this book as a basis for dealing with them. However, if problems continue and you find yourself dealing with the same person and issues repeatedly, you will want to consider the recommendations that follow.

First

Do use and apply the key ideas recommended in this text. They can and will make a difference:

> Acknowledgment
>
> Appreciation
>
> Recognition
>
> Reward

Remember, difficult people are hurting inside. They have low self-worth and overall may need quite a bit of positive attention. REALLY difficult people may need more positive attention than you or your team members can give, but what you CAN give will help.

Remember to use

The Seven Keys to Understanding and Working with Difficult People

Self-Awareness

Self-worth

Self-Confidence

Self-Control

Honesty

Kindness

Positivity

I am often asked how to deal with a particularly difficult case (and asked to come in and work with someone who is seen as pervasively difficult by others). Typically at this stage everyone knows there is a problem, and everyone, even the 'difficult' person*, wants to find a solution.

*Important: Keep in mind that most difficult people do not see themselves as being difficult, even when there is a good bit of evidence and more than a few people who may attest to the fact.

> I am reminded of a situation I was called in to help mediate. The organization that hired me was concerned about the head of a major team that had received many complaints about her style and interactions with others. When I entered the room and saw her for the first time, I was literally almost blown away by the woman's rigidity and what I would almost have to call the 'fierceness' of her demeanor. This was just by seeing her from across the room.

> After talking with her briefly I realized two key points:

>> She did not have the least conception of how she was coming across to others.

>> At heart she was a nice person who was devastated by the accusations and concerns that had arisen.

Which raises another important truth – most people do not want to be seen negatively, or be seen as being difficult.

People usually have very good reasons for how they behave, at least from their perspective. They don't understand why other people misinterpret their words and actions. When asked about their difficultness, they tend to point away from themselves and suggest that everyone else is being difficult.

When entering this type of situation/meeting, you can expect the person to be very resistant and not very happy. If you have worked with them before on specific concerns, then this may be a more serious and in-depth attempt to resolve recurring issues. The following can work well as a preliminary step to get them on the same page as you. It is important for you to stay calm, in-control and to avoid negativity/blame as much as is feasible under the circumstances.

> "Kelly, you know why you are here. Concerns we have addressed before seem to be a continuing issue. I want to work with you on a solution that is best for all concerned, including keeping you as a productive, quality member of this team."

Obviously what you say initially will depend on the specific circumstances, however, try to offer some support and encouragement right from the get-go. Don't expect Kelly to ease defensives at this stage or jump onto your bandwagon.

> "You know that I feel it is very important to have a team that works well together and gets the job done. I have spoken often about the things that I feel are key to our success. I believe you feel the same way, but there are concerns that we do need to address so we can get beyond some of the issues that have been brought up by others in relationship to your work on this team. Here, please take a careful look at this list,"

At this point I would hand them a list of "The Seven Keys to Understanding and Working with Difficult People," with the title removed. After they had looked at it long enough to digest it thoroughly I would continue. (You can generate your own 'go-to' list for this purpose.)

> "How do you feel about this list? Is there anything on this list that you don't agree with; that you feel you can't live with?"

You will have to see how they respond, but typically people do not have any problems with this list. They actually like it and see its importance. However, you may get a good bit of, "Well, this is just great for me, but what about Steve and Beth. They sure don't live up to this," and so on. Direct the discussion back to them.

"Kelly, you know I work with everyone on this team and I don't want this to be about blame. I want this to be about how I can help you and how you can take responsibility for what you do and say and how that impacts others. The past is past. This list is about what you, and I, can do to help you make a positive difference with everyone."

From this point on I would emphasize the importance of self-awareness and how we come across to others. I would try to give Kelly an exercise and goal to spend the next week working on being aware of how he/she applies one or more of these keys in their daily life, specifically asking him/her to watch carefully how his/her interactions with others go.

Probably the most important aspect of working with a really difficult personality is getting them to self-observe and helping them move away from their tendency to judge others. This technique may or may not work depending on the personality, but it does get at part of the heart of the matter.

There are many ways to address serious concerns. This is one that has worked well for me. You may choose a far different course that is based around the values and qualities you feel are most important relevant to a particular situation and to your team.

The next level

If, in spite of all your efforts and the efforts of team members, things don't improve, you may have to let the person know firmly and directly that their behavior is unacceptable and that continued problems could result in serious consequences. Again, I would handle this as judiciously and kindly as possible, but ultimately they need to understand what is important to their success as a member of your team.

"Kelly, we have met a number of times about issues that have risen with other team members. It is important that you understand the seriousness of this problem. I am willing to continue to work with you on making a difference, and I am willing to offer whatever support you feel you may need to help improve what is happening. However, you need to know that any further concerns will be directly addressed on your evaluation…"

Be willing to talk openly about what the issues are and the changes you want to see, efforts they need to make, etc. Be sure to let them know that you are documenting everything.

Be aware that they may be highly defensive, angry, and blaming. If at this stage you feel it would be important, bring in someone from Human Resources (or someone from another appropriate work venue)* to sit in on the session. Apprise them of what has transpired to date, what documentation you have, and what you intend to say.

*Some businesses may have specific procedures and recommendations for this type of meeting. Check with Human Resources and/or your boss for additional information and advice.

Serious personality concerns

It is possible, perhaps even likely, that in your career as a manager and leader that you will eventually have to deal with a person who has serious psychological concerns. Unless you are a licensed counselor, trained in diagnoses and mandated by your business to act as a professional counselor, DO NOT try to diagnose or treat a person who is having major concerns at work. Get help.

Find out whatever resources are available and get advice on how to handle the situation. Document everything and try to make sure that this doesn't get swept under the table. Your team and your career may be at stake.

Other serious issues

There are a variety of issues which might arise that can cause problems within your team and between team players. Alcoholism and drug addiction can play a role in serious difficulties at work.

Understand the problem as thoroughly as you can

Work with your boss, Human Resources, and/or other appropriate departments

Work with the person/persons involved within the parameters of guidelines and procedures set by your place of work.

Leadership

Leadership is about making the best of every circumstance. Sometimes things are a bit tougher than we would like, but you are an intelligent, knowledgeable, and caring leader of your people. Make a difference by being willing to make a difference. Your people will appreciate it.

Questions and Ideas for Contemplation

Really difficult behaviors can be draining on everyone. Be sure to take care of yourself and take care of your team players. Keep up the positivity in spite of whatever negativity may be dragging people down. This can help as much to resolve the situation as anything else.

Chapter 31

Leading By Example

Much of this book is about leadership. How you work as a manager, and how you work with your people make all the difference in the world in what you will face on a day-to-day basis. Difficulties will happen; problems will occur; people will need to work through issues. You have the knowledge, skills, and tools to be successful. Keep in mind, though, that whatever stage you set will influence how good the play is.

Walk the Walk

Your key values and the qualities that inspire you will be noticed when you live them each and every day. People notice. They notice far more than we realize.

> If you spend most of your time in the office dealing with e-mails and phone calls – they will notice and wonder why they don't count more

> If you give up quality time with your people to attend one more meeting that may or may not be so 'necessary' – they will feel you have let them down

> If you hide things and don't make an effort to communicate with them on a regular basis (see over-communicating – Chapters 9 and 20) – they will wonder what is up; rumors and a lot of behind the scenes stuff you don't want going on will start up.

> If you don't go to bat for them when things get difficult – they will start to question your integrity and honesty; they will wonder if you really care.

Bring the fundamental you, the person you would be proud to sponsor, always to the fore and you will have a team that responds with vitality and effort to what needs to be done.

Talk the Talk

Don't just leave it at walking the walk; you also have to let everyone know, as often as possible, what you value.

> Tell them what is most important to their success, the team's success, the businesses' success, and yes, your success. After all, it is all tied together.
>
> Tell them what you are passionate about
>
> Let them know what you admire in others
>
> Let them know what you expect of yourself and of them
>
> Let them know at every opportunity

Then you will have a team that you can be proud of.

> The game you play is best judged by how well
>
> you help your teammates play
>
> (paraphrased from Bill Russell, Basketball Player).

"When you are in a hole, stop digging." (Molly Ivins)

Take responsibility and find solutions. When you take on the mantle of leadership, you accept a tremendous amount of responsibility. Yes, the mess you just entered may not be of your making, but YOU can make a difference. YOU are that good. It does take some time and patience. Probably some sacrifices. Maybe a bit of stress and some long days and nights, but you will get there. That is why they hired YOU.

Go get 'em tiger.

Best,

Joe Koob

Appendix I

Handling Employee Evaluations

Evaluation Processes

If you have been a manager for any period of time, you have probably struggled with one or more company evaluation processes. Unfortunately many of these measures are poorly designed, and even those that are reasonably well-designed and set up to provide constructive feedback, are rarely implemented well. There are typically far too many fingers in the pie, and the value, if there was any to start with, is lost by in-fighting on details.

Process problems

Quotas

Even companies that claim they don't have quotas or 'strict' quotas, usually do. They try to make it seem like they don't on the surface for political reasons, but the truth is, that when push comes to shove, the managers are forced to pigeon-hole everyone into neat little packages of 'quality.'

Length

BIG company evaluation processes have become incredibly cumbersome. Leaders who manage large groups find themselves overwhelmed one or more times a year with 'evaluation packages' that take days to fill out and revise.

Frequency

Two, three, four times a year and each time a 'packet' of materials for each employee! Has someone up above forgotten you actually have mandated performance criteria yourself?

Efficacy

Today the purpose of the whole evaluation process at many large companies seems to be aimed at giving bonuses and raises and little else. Unfortunately, bonuses and raises have become such an ingrained, expected part of the compensation that all employees at every level receive something (often quite a bit) even though their performance may have been abysmal. [Need we look very far when we see Presidents and CEOs garnering huge bonuses while their companies' stock tanks?]

These concerns are the most obvious. There are often many confusing and ambiguous elements to evaluation process that defy even Human Resources' ability to understand and elucidate them.

What can you do?

You are leading a team – a team that you are striving to make an effective, competent, and quality-producing department in your company. Yet, you are facing the ominous (yes, ominous) task of evaluating each member of your team with these many disturbing caveats as part of the evaluation process. Can you succeed? Can you come out of this with only a bit of egg smear on your face? Can you make a positive difference, somehow, with your troops in spite of the inherent problems of the process itself? Read on.

Succeeding with Quotas

I have been an antagonist of quota systems for as long as I can remember. From my standpoint as a coach, they set up outstanding leaders to always have a measure of failure about what they do. What incentive does a new leader have to deliver an outstanding team effort on a consistent, year-in-year-out basis, when he/she is forced to relegate a certain percentage of team members into the 'lowest' pool every year?

Here is a true story:

I was in a system once where for several years they announced a merit bonus (in this particular business, bonuses were not common). Department heads were told to place their team members in three pools, High, Middle, and Low. This was the typical mimic of the 'Bell-shaped-Curve' distribution.

Regardless of the quality of their team players – good or bad – the department heads had to have 20% in the low pool, 60% in the middle pool, and 20% in the high pool.

The result?

Everyone on the low pool felt really lousy. The people in the middle pool felt thankful they weren't in the low pool, but were definitely not happy about where they were placed. The people in the high pool felt good about 'the honor,' but many felt guilty about being placed above their compatriots.

Get this – all of this effort and the resulting de-motivation of the majority of the workforce was for fifty dollars in bonus for the middle pool and one hundred dollars for the top pool. Yes, that's $50.00 and $100.00 (and no, I'm not two hundred years old).

Even if the incentives are much greater – thousands and tens of thousands of dollars – the demoralizing effects of quota systems are still there.

What can you do?

I have always been of the mindset that if I have created an outstanding team, I am going to fight for them with everything I have to negate the quota system and rate them based on their performance only. However, even if you feel this strongly, you might be backed into a corner and forced to make a decision to place your people in levels.

I have seen this task approached from a variety of perspectives by good managers:

An alternating system, where your people are placed in levels based simply on what year it is

Placing retiring or leaving personnel in the lowest slots, to avoid placing any ongoing team members in them

Placing the newest personnel in the lowest spots (and sometimes placing those with the most longevity in the highest spots).

There aren't any great choices.

My recommendation – be open and honest about the system and how it works; and then work with maximum input from all your personnel to find the best possible approach. Most importantly, evaluate your personnel honestly and let them know why decisions have been made one way or another. Hiding behind a process is the worst thing you can do.

Length

Some evaluation processes are unconscionably long and tedious. Here are some key concepts for handling them most efficaciously:

> Organization is key: make sure you have all your ducks in a row before starting to work on the evaluations. If you don't, you will be scrambling for information. Insist on timelines and data from subordinates.

> Make sure that last year's evaluation is the jumping off place for this year's and sets up the evaluation for next year. When you are this organized, all subsequent evaluation processes become somewhat easier.

> Write (fill-in-the-blanks) from a, 'this-is-how-I-feel,' basic gut reaction basis (assuming you have done all the organization and reading of data ahead of time). Far too many managers I have coached spend oodles of time pondering the right choice of words, perseverating over details, etc. My recommendation is to get it down on paper, then go back and tweak it when you are completely done. It takes far less time to do it this way and you end up with a good global perspective of this particular evaluation before you make any adjustments. It is also, I feel, a far more honest appraisal when done this way.

> Back up everything – you don't want to have to do this again. Make sure your previous year's files are saved and available for the next year.

> Be honest – people appreciate your honesty and openness. The less that is hidden, the better. People want to know what they need to do to improve.

> Work toward making the process more efficient. This type of bureaucracy CAN be changed, but you have to be willing to make the effort. If you hate the system, work to change it.

Frequency

If you face more than one lengthy evaluation process a year, your best tool is to maintain detailed records of each process. It will make the next one far easier. Once you have established a solid, open evaluation process and documentation for your team, you will be able to jump off of that for all subsequent evaluations

Your next best tool is to stay on top of your employee evaluations year round (see below, "The Only Evaluation Process that Works")

Efficacy

YOU make the choices in handling evaluations processes that make a difference to YOUR people. Make the process as open, honest, and team-building as you can within the parameters set by the business. The truth is, you can always build-in constructive and positive feedback that will help your team members feel better about what they have done and what they need to do in the future.

Make their improvement and advancement your goal and they will know that you are there for them, and not just going through the motions for the company.

The only Evaluation Process that Works

The only evaluation system that works is one in which you, as manager and leader, commit to the betterment of your personnel and team. You do this by making evaluation an ongoing process, not a once a year, company policy.

There are many ways to do this, but the foundation is an open, honest approach that lets people know on a daily, weekly, monthly basis how they are doing, what can be improved, and what they are doing well.

Keep in mind these key tools:

Acknowledgement

Appreciation

Recognition

Reward

You have the power to make a difference regardless of what formal evaluative processes the company requires. Make a difference by being a caring leader.

You have to let them know in some way, because they won't know otherwise. And what people don't know, creates angst. Make it a habit to give your people feedback frequently so they can continue the good work they are doing and improve on the things that need improving.

The Final Word - Honesty

Evaluating your people, and they are only **your people** if you care, is one of the harder jobs you face as a manager and leader. When push comes to shove, honesty is the best policy. When you couple honesty with kindness and as much positivity and support that you can add, you will be building quality players on your team.

This is especially true when it comes to formal evaluation processes. Regardless of the specific process, the forms you have to fill out, and the quotas that must be met, YOU set the stage for whether these evaluations will help people grow and advance or whether they present a confusing message to your team members.

The only way you can ensure an even playing field, and a motivated, productive team, is to be honest within the parameters of the process you are dealing with and to let your team players know how and why you have made the decisions that you have. If you don't, they will question everything you have said and done during the year and they will question your integrity.

Honesty means telling the truth, and the truth includes:

A fair appraisal of their work based on goals and other formal criteria

An appraisal that, in the final analysis, matches the feedback you have been providing them throughout the year

The courage to offer them constructive criticism and support for what they need to work on

Sharing with them the ins and outs of the evaluation process and why and how decisions are made

An improvement/development plan and the support and encouragement to help implement it

No one likes criticism. But they do appreciate honesty, because when they know what is going on and why, the ball is placed in their hands and it is then their choice to play the game well or not.

Honesty, coupled with kindness, is ultimately empowering to all.

Appendix II

Being in control

The object of paying attention to yourself is not to control others, **but to be in control of yourself**. At the root, this means not giving over your emotions, your power, your behavior (reaction) to another person. It has to do with Assertiveness.

Assertiveness is, fundamentally, being able to stand up for yourself in a positive way.

Staying in control of you

Several years ago when I was working at the VA Medical Center in San Diego, I was fortunate to work with Dr. John McQuaid. In the course of my writing several manuals for drug and alcohol group therapy, John introduced me to something he had written for use with the patients. I had also pursued the same reasoning as his in my book, *A Perfect Day: Guide for a Better Life*. After I read it, I liked John's approach a lot. As with many good ideas this one is simple and easy to remember:

>   Catch It
>
>   Check It
>
>   Change It

While the concept isn't new, the "**3 C's**" makes it easy to remember.

Paying Attention equals "Catch it"

The first step in gaining and maintaining self-control in a difficult situation is to **Catch** yourself. By paying attention to your emotions, what you are thinking, and the reaction you are about to have (action you will take), you set yourself up for making a choice.

Choices...

...are everything in difficult situations. Rather than buying into the other person's mania or difficulty and immediately reacting, you can now be who you want to be – who you choose to be. You make the choices. The other person doesn't 'control' you by dragging you into their emotionality.

Check it

While this may seem like the obvious next step, It is not always so clear cut. You want everything about this difficult situation you find yourself in to be very clear for you. **Checking it** helps you set up making different choices than you would normally make.

Take a close look at your feelings, your thoughts, and your soon to be reaction. Is this really how you want to feel, think, and react?

The bomb didn't go off?

The simple act of checking these inner workings of your mind and body does a very important thing. It sets up a pause in the proceedings. That pause means you are still in control. It will also, very likely, puzzle the heck out of the difficult person. He wants and is waiting for, the expected reaction from you. When you don't explode, the situation no longer fits the 'norm.' Behaviors can and very likely will change as a result.

Change it

Then you have the choice of redirecting yourself and the situation. As you will find out, this makes all the difference in the world in dealing with difficult people.

Remember

> **Catch it**: are you paying attention to yourself?

> **Check it**: is this really how you want to be?

> **Change it**: make a different choice

It is important to pay attention to how the difficult person you are dealing with reacts to this new turn of events, too.

What kind of attitude DO you want to bring to a difficult situation?

Think of difficult situations you have been in recently and imagine taking these extra moments to stay in control. Can you see yourself making other choices?

Try practicing **Catch it, Check it, Change it** in a variety of situations this week. They don't have to be difficult situations. Just see if you can get the hang of it. You might be surprised at how much control you suddenly have – control of yourself and the choices you make.

Appendix III

Annotated Bibliography

Works by Dr. Joseph Koob

Books with a Business Focus

Business Trilogy: Dealing with Change

Difficult Situations - Dealing with Change

Difficult situations can certainly produce a great deal of angst and as a result, difficult people. From my own long personal experience, I know that when things are tough, I can get much more difficult than normal. Those are the times when I know I need to deal with my own stuff.

Honoring Work and Life: 99 Words for Leaders to Live By

This book provides a foundation of key ideas that focus on Leadership (and Personal) qualities, attributes, and behaviors that honor not only our work but our life. It is my firm belief that true leaders work to serve their fellow employees, their team, their company, their customers, as well as their families and friends. This is about understanding and working on those attributes that make great leaders.

Leaders Managing Change

Leaders Managing Change is about understanding and dealing with the ongoing stresses of constant change in the business world today, but most importantly it is about leadership. When I thought about the concerns that are a regular part of high turnover rates, leadership changes, acquisitions and mergers, and the myriad of other transitions businesses face today, the focus came down to leadership. Good leaders get things done. This book focuses on knowledgeable leadership, i.e. what you need to know to help you deal with change as a leader. It presumes you are already inspired, good, intelligent, and practical. This book is about making a difference.

Business Trilogy: Succeeding at Work

Dealing with Difficult Coworkers

This work is one that based on my research is a needed addition to the difficult people literature. There are a number of books available that discuss difficult people in the workplace, but do not focus specifically on coworkers. There are different dynamics between bosses and employees, employees and their peers, and employees with their bosses. The emphasis here is on helping people solve the difficulties they have at work with someone who is relatively speaking a 'coworker,' or 'colleague,' in other words, someone whose 'rank' or 'job' is roughly on the same level as theirs.

Succeeding with Difficult Bosses

Have a tough boss? This is a practical, in-the-trenches approach to succeeding with a difficult authority figure. So much of our appreciation and success at work seems to have to do with who our boss is – as a manager (good or bad), as a leader (one who inspires or does not), and, most importantly, as a person (does he/she care). What we do care the most about in a person who is above us in the chain of command is their willingness (or not) to acknowledge, appreciate, and recognize who we are and the effort we put forth.

Managing Difficult Employees

This book is first and foremost about leadership. What can I do as a manager and leader to create a work environment that fosters positive personnel development? In other words, <u>preventive maintenance</u> – avoiding difficult people concerns and difficult situations through competent management and inspired leadership. It is also about the knowledge you need, and the skills you can learn to be able to deal with people concerns that are present or that may arise?

Dealing with Difficult Customers

(for Employees, Companies, and Customer Service Personnel)

This book is all about putting the gamut of customer relations and interactions into a perspective that is workable, livable, and supports you, the customer contact person, throughout.

While many businesses do provide extensive customer relations training, the focus is often fairly one way – aimed at keeping business. We present you with extensive insight and knowledge about the customer's perspective, what you need to know as a company representative to fulfill your job, the internal and external support you need, and the tools and skills to communicate effectively with difficult customers.

Caring for Difficult Patients: A Guide for Nursing Professionals

I believe that the Nursing profession is one of the most admired in America. We think of Nurses as professional: that is, they have a knowledge base and skill set that is unique and valued – the quality of their work is important to them; and we think of Nurses as people who care about their patients – they are concerned with our well-being when we are under their care. These considerations are the focal point for discussing how to best deal with difficult patients.

Books with a Personal Focus

Understanding and Working with Difficult People

We believe this book presents the most comprehensive material available about being successful with difficult people. This book is designed to be a practical, accessible introduction to the very broad topic of dealing with difficult people/difficult behaviors. Since every difficult situation is different, the focus here will be on building a basic understanding of how you interact with difficult people, what makes difficult people tick, and the most fundamental skills you can bring to the table to help change these encounters for the better.

ME! A Difficult Person?

This is second of our signature books. This book focuses on learning more about yourself. Most of us are occasionally difficult or seen as difficult by others. This may simply be a matter of different perspectives, or it may mean that we have some inner work to do. This course is concerned with understanding more about how you come across to others, and understanding more about who you are as a person. It is also concerned with self-improvement – making changes that will help make your interactions with others significantly better, and that will bring you more peace, comfort, and joy in your life.

Dealing with Difficult Strangers

Being successful in difficult situations with strangers is all about what you can bring to the situation. You will find a tremendous amount of useful information and skills included in this book that can make a significant difference in how you approach difficult strangers, how you feel as a result of these difficult encounters, and how you can emerge without a negative experience having ruined your day.

Difficult Spouses? Improving and Saving Your Relationship with Your Significant Other

Are you having difficulties in your current relationship? Facing a divorce? Newly divorced and trying to understand what happened and what you could have done about it? We feel this book has value not only for couples who are simply having difficulties in their relationships with their significant others; those facing divorce, recently divorced couples; and for people entering new relationships. The focus is on developing the knowledge, skills, and tools to help your relationship be successful.

Succeeding with Difficult Professors (and Tough Courses)

A course for college students at all levels. What you need to know to make the most of your college career. This course has two main sections: "Getting along with Difficult Professors," and "Succeeding in Tough Classes." The first section will discuss ideas and skills you can use to get through personal difficulties with professors. The second section will focus on techniques, study skills, and approaches that will help you get the grades you want.

Guiding Children

Guiding and working with children is on the mind of every parent. This book focuses on skills and tools to help you as a parent provide the best possible environment for your child's development by avoiding difficulties through intelligent upbringing. This book is not only about helping you to guide your children through concerns that arise, but it is even more about enjoying your children. They do grow up, much faster than we expect. Take advantage of the tremendous joy they can bring into your life and the vast understanding of life that they provide. You will be glad you did.

Bibliography

Difficult People Materials

Axelrod, A and Holtje, J., *201 Ways to Deal with Difficult People*, McGraw-Hill, New York, 1997.

Bell, A. and Smith, D., *Winning with Difficult People*, Barron's, New York, 1997

Bramson, Robert M., *Coping with Difficult Bosses*, Fireside, New York, 1992.

Bramson, Robert M., *Coping with Difficult People*, Anchor Press, New York, 1981.

Braunstein, Barbara, *How to Deal with Difficult People*, Skillpath Publications, Mission, KS, 1994. [Tapes]

Brinkman, R. and Kirschner, R., *Dealing with People You Can't Stand*, McGraw-Hill, New York, 1994.

Carter, Jay, *Nasty Bosses: How to STOP BEING HURT by them without stooping to THEIR level*, McGraw-Hill, New York, 2004.

Case, Gary and Rhoades-Baum, *How to Handle Difficult Customers*, Help Deck Institute, Colorado Springs, 1994.

Cava, Roberta, *Dealing with Difficult People: How to Deal with Nasty Customers, Demanding Bosses and Annoying Co-workers*, Firefly Books, Buffalo, NY, 2004.

Cava, Roberta, *difficult people: How to Deal with Impossible clients, Bosses, and Employees*, Firefly Books, Buffalo, NY, 1990.

Cavaiola, A. And Lavender, N., *Toxic Coworkers: How to Deal with Dysfunctional People on the Job*, New Harbinger Publications, Oakland, CA, 2000.

Costello, Andrew, *How to Deal with Difficult People*, Ligori Publications, Liguri, MI, 1980.

Crowe, Sandra, *Since Strangling Isn't An Option*, Perigee, New York, 1999.

Diehm, William, *How to Get Along with Difficult People*, Broadman Press, Nashville, 1992.

Felder, Leonard, *Does Someone Treat You Badly? How to Handle Brutal Bosses, Crazy Coworkers...and Anyone Else Who Drives You Nuts*, Berkley Books, NY, 1993.

First, Michael, Ed., *Diagnostic and Statistical Manual for Mental Disorders*, 4th Edition, American Psychiatric Asso.,Washington, 1994.

Friedman, Paul, *How to Deal with Difficult People*, SkillPath Publications, Mission, KS, 1994.

Gill, Lucy, *How to Work with Just About Anyone*, Fireside, New York, 1999.

Griswold, Bob, *Coping with Difficult and Negative People and Personal Magnetism*, Effective Learning Systems, Inc., Edina, MN. [Tape]

Holloway, Andy, "Bad Boss Blues," *Canadian Business*, 24 Oct 2004.

Hoover, John, *How to Work for an Idiot: Survive & Thrive Without Killing Your Boss*, Career Press, Princeton, NJ, 2004.

Jones, Katina, *Succeeding with Difficult People*, Longmeadow Press, Stamford, CT, 1992.

Keating, Charles, *Dealing with Difficult People*, Paulist Press, New York, 1984.

Littauer, Florence, *How to Get Along with Difficult People*, Harvest House, Eugene, 1984.

Lloyd, Ken, *Jerks at Work: How to Deal with People Problems and Problem People*, Career Press, Franklin Lakes, NJ, 1999

Lundin, W. and Lundin, J., *When Smart People Work for Dumb Bosses: How to Survive in a Crazy and Dysfunctional Workplace*, McGraw-Hill, New York, 1998.

Markham, Ursula, *How to deal with Difficult people*, Thorsons, London, 1993.

Meier, Paul, *Don't Let Jerks Get the Best of You: Advice for Dealing with Difficult People*, Thomas Nelson, Nashville, 1993.

Namie, G. and Namie, R., *the Bully at Work*, Sourcebooks, Inc., Naperville, IL, 2000.

Osbourne, Christina, *Dealing with Difficult People*, DK, London, 2002.

Oxman, Murray, *The How to Easily Handle Difficult People, Success Without Stress*, Morro Bay, CA, 1997.

Perkins, Betty, *Lion Taming: The Courage to Deal with Difficult People Including Yourself*, Tzedakah Publications, Scramento, 1995.

Rosen, Mark, *Thank You for Being Such A Pain: Spiritual Guidance for Dealing with Difficult People*, Three Rivers Press, New York, 1998.

Segal, Judith, *Getting Them to See It Your Way: Dealing with Difficult and Challenging People*, Lowell House, Los Angeles, 2000.

Solomon, Muriel, *Working with Difficult People*, Prentice Hall, Englewood Cliffs,1990.

Toropov, Brandon, *The Complete Idiot's Guide to Getting Along with Difficult People*, Alpha Books, New York, 1997.

Toropov, Brandon, *Manager's Guide to Dealing with Difficult People*, Prentice Hall, Paramus, NJ, 1997.

Turecki, Stanley, *The Difficult Child*, Bantam Books, NY, 1989.

Weiner, David L., *Power Freaks: Dealing with Them in the Workplace or Anywhere*, Prometheus Books, Amherst, New York, 2002

Weiss, Donald, *How to Deal with Difficult People*, Amacon, New York, 1987.

Recommended Readings

Dewey, John, *Democracy and Education*, Norwood Press, Norwood, MA, 1916.

Dewey, John, *Education and Experience*, Kappa Delta Pi Publications, Macmillian, New York, 1938.

Dyer, Wayne, *Pulling Your Own Strings*, Funk and Wagnalls, New York, 1978.

Dyer, Wayne, *Your Erroneous Zones*, Funk and Wagnalls, New York, 1976.

Dyer, Wayne, *Your Sacred Self*, Harper, New York, 1995.

Guraik, David B., Editor, *Webster's New World Dictionary*, World Publishing, New York, 1972.

Heinlein, Robert, *Time Enough for Love*, New English Library, New York, 1974.

Hesse, Hermann, *Narcissus and Goldmund*, Bantam, New York, 1971.

James, M, and Jongeward, D. *Born to Win*, Addison-Wesley, 1971.

Koob, Joseph, *A Perfect Day: Guide for A Better Life*, NEJS Publications, Lawton, OK, 1998.

Parrott, Thomas Marc, Ed., *Shakespeare: Twenty-three Plays and the Sonnets*, Charles Scribner's Sons, Washington, D.C., 1938.

Pirsig, Robert, *Zen and the Art of Motorcycle Maintenance*, Bantam, New York, 1980.

Rand, Ayn, *Atlas Shrugged*, Signet Books, New York, 1957.

Redman, Ben Ray, Editor, *The Portable Voltaire*, Viking Press, New York, 1949.

Books and other works on Change and Leadership

Bolles, Richard N., *What Color is Your Parachute?* Ten Speed Press, Berkeley, CA, 1987.

Bridges, William, *Managing Transitions: Making the Most of Change*, Perseus Books, Cambridge, 1991.

Bridges, William, *Transitions: Making Sense of Life's Changes*, Perseus Books, Cambridge, 1980.

Buckingham, Marcus, & Coffman, Curt, *First, Break All the Rules: What the World's Greatest Managers Do Differently*, Simon and Schuster, New York, 1999.

Collins, J., and Porras, J., *Built to Last: Successful Habits of Visionary Companies*, Harper Business, NY, 2001.

Collins, Jim, *Good TO Great: Why Some Companies Make the Leap...and Others Don't*, Harper Business, NY, 2001.

Cooper, Robert and Sawaf, Ayman, *Executive EQ: Emotional Intelligence in Leadership & Organizations*, Grisset/Putnam, New York, 1996.

Crane, Thomas, *The Heart of Coaching*, FTA Press, San Diego, 1998.

Deits, Bob, Life *After Loss: A Personal Guide Dealing with Death, Divorce, Job Change and Relocation*, Fisher Books, Tucson, 1988.

Dominhguez, Linda R., *How to Shine at Work*, McGraw Hill, 2003.

Drucker, Peter F., *Managing in a Time of Great Change*, Truman Talley Books, NY, 1995.

Evard, Beth L. And Gipple, Craig A., *Managing Business Change for Dummies*, Hungry Minds, Inc., NY,2001.

Farson, Richard and Keyes, Ralph, *Whoever Makes the Most Mistakes Wins: The Paradox of Innovation*, Free Press, NY, 2002.

Fortgang, Laura Berman, *Take Yourself to the Top: The Secrets of America's #1 Career Coach*, Warner Books, New York, 1998.

Gates, Bill, *Business @ the Speed of Thought: Succeeding in the Digital Economy*, Warner Books, New York, 1999.

Gerstner, Jr., Louis, V, *Who Says Elephants Can't Dance? Leading a Great Enterprise Through Dramatic Change*, HarperBusiness, New York, 2002.

Going Through Bereavement–When a loved one dies, Langeland Memorial Chapel, Kalamazoo, MI.

Grieve, Bradly T., *The Blue Day Book: A Lesson in Cheering Yourself Up*, Andrews McMeel Publishing, Kansas City, 2000.

Goldratt, Eliyahu M., *Critical Chain*, North River Press, Great Barrington, MA, 1997.

Hammer, Michael and Champy, James, *Reengineering the Corporation: A Manifesto for Business Revolution, HarperBusiness*, New York, 1993.

Hoffer, Eric, *The Ordeal of Change*, Harper & Row, NY, 1952.

Jeffreys, J. Shep. *Coping with Workplace Change: Dealing with Loss and Grief*, Crisp Productions, Menlo Park, CA, 1995.

Johnson, Spencer, *Who Moved My Cheese*, G. P. Putnam, New York, 1998.

Kanter, Rosabeth Moss, *The Change Masters: Innovation & Entrepreneurship in the American Corporation*, Simon & Schuster, New York, 1983.

Kelley, Robert, *How to be a Star at Work: Nine Breakthrough Strategies You Need to Succeed*, Random House, New York, 1998.

Koob, Joseph E. II, *Difficult Situations: Dealing with Change*, NEJS Publications, Saline, MI, 2004.

Kotter, John P, *Leading Change*, Harvard Business School Press, Boston, 1996.

Kotter, John P, *The Leadership Factor*, Free Press, New York, 1988.

Kouzes, J. and Posner, B., *Credibility: How Leaders Gain and Lose it; Why People Demand it*, Jossey-Bass Publishers, San Francisco, 1993.

Kuster, Elizabeth, *Exorcising Your Ex*, Fireside, New York, 1996.

Leonard, George, *Mastery: The Keys to Success and Long-term Fulfillment*, Plume, NY 1992.

Lunden, Joan, and Cagan, Andrea, *A Bend in the Road is Not the End of the Road,* William Morrow, New York, 1998.

Maxwell, John C., *The 21 Indispensible Qualities of Leadership: Becoming the Person Others Will Want to Follow*, Thomas Nelson Publishers, Nashville, 1999.

Maxwell, John C., *The 17 Indisputable Laws of Teamwork: Embrace them and Empower Your Team*, Thomas Nelson Publishers, Nashville, 2001.

Maxwell, John C., *21 Irrefutable Laws of Leadership*, Thomas Nelson, Inc., Nashville, 1998.

Milwid, Beth, *Working With Men: Professional Women Talk About Power, Sexuality, and Ethics*, Beyond Words, Kingsport, TN, 1990.

McKay, Harvey, *Swim with the Sharks: Without Being Eaten Alive*, William Morrow Co., New York, 1988.

Messer, Bonnie J., *Dealing with Change*, Abington Press, 1996.

Montalbo, Thomas, *The Power of Eloquence: Magic Key to Success in Public Speaking*, Prentive-Hall, Englewood Cliffs, N.J., 1984.

Pasternack, Bruce and Viscio, Albert, *The Centerless Corporation: A New Model for Transforming Your Organization for Growth and Prosperity*, Fireside, New York, 1998.

Peters, Tom, *The Circle of Innovation: You Can't Shrink Your Way to Greatnness*, Vintage Books, New York, 1999.

Peters, Tom, *Liberation Management: Necessary Disorganization for the Nanosecond Nineties*, Faucett Columbine, New York, 1992.

Peters, Tom, and Waterman, Robert, *In Search of Excellence: Lessons from America's Best-Run Companies*, Harper & Row, New York, 1982.

Peters, Tom, and Austin, Nancy, *A Passion for Excellence: The Leadership Difference*, Random House, New York, 1985.

Peters, Tom, *The Pursuit of WOW! Every Person's Guide to Topsy-Turvy Times*, Vintage Books, New York, 1994.

Peters, Tom, *Professional Service Firm 50: Fifty Ways to Transform Your "Department" into a Professional Service Firm whose Trademarks are Passion and Excellence*, Alfred A. Knopf, 1999.

Peters, Tom, *Re-imagine! Business Excellence in a Disruptive Age*, DK, London, 2003.

Peters, Tom, *Thriving on Chaos: Handbook for a Management Revolution*, Alfred Knopf, New York, 1987

Popcorn, Faith, *EVEolutuon: The Eight Truths of Marketing to Women*, Hyperion Books, 2001.

Smith, Hyrum W. The *10 Natural Laws of Successful Time and Life Management: Proven Strategies for Increased Productivity and Inner Peace*, Warner Books, New York, 1994.

Talbot, Kay, *The Ten Biggest Myths About Grief*, Abbey Press, St. Meinrad, IN, 2000.

Waterman, Robert H., Jr., *The Renewal Factor: How The Best Get And Keep The Competitive Edge*, Bantam, New York, 1986.

Whitmore, John, *Coaching for Performance*, Nicholas Brealey Publishing, London, 1999.